Every Day is Saturday

A Christian Guide to a Fantastic Retirement

L. James & Jackie Harvey

CPH
SAINT LOUIS

Cover illustration by David Wink.

Copyright © 2000 L. James Harvey and Jackie Harvey
Published by Concordia Publishing House
3558 S. Jefferson Avenue, St. Louis, MO 63118-3968

Manufactured in the United States of America

Library of Congress Cataloging-in-Publication Data

Harvey, L. James, 1930-
    Every day is Saturday : a Christian guide to a fantastic retirement
/L. James Harvey and Jackie Harvey.
    p. cm.
    Includes bibliographical references.
    ISBN 0-570-05250-5
    1. Retirees—Religious life. 2. Retirement—Religious aspects—Christianity.
I. Harvey, Jackie. II. Title.
    BV4596.R47 H37 2001
    248.8'5—dc21

                              00-010076

1 2 3 4 5 6 7 8 9 10   09 08 07 06 05 04 03 02 01 00

This book is dedicated to the people we have met along our pathway through life who have meant so much to us.

To our children, Linda, Doug, Leslie, and Lisa.

We are grateful to our parents and to our brothers and sisters, including our in-laws.

Our early lives were shaped to a large extent by teachers, coaches, and classmates at Ottawa Hills High School in Grand Rapids, Michigan, and at Hope College in Holland, Michigan.

Our life was richly blessed by the players, students, and friends we came to know at Bellflower Christian High School (now Valley Christian) in California where we first established our roots after college.

We have been blessed with great brothers and sisters in Christ wherever we settled in Michigan, California, Illinois, and Maryland.

We also have been blessed with wonderful professional colleagues at Hope, Harper, and Prince George's Colleges, and McManis Associates and the Prince George's Correctional Facility.

As we look back, we realize ever more keenly just how much these wonderful people have enriched our lives. One of the great blessings of retirement is that we have the time to renew these marvelous friendships and to spend time with those to whom we owe so much and who have so enlightened and improved our lives. We regret we do not have space here to list everyone to whom we refer. You know who you are. To you we dedicate this book with our heartfelt thanks.

ACKNOWLEDGMENTS

Many people have been instrumental in helping us put this book together. We would like to express our sincere thanks to them.

To the Rev. Donald Fulton and his wife, Meridian, for reviewing the manuscript, making constructive suggestions, particularly to the chapter on faith, and for their constant prayers and encouragement.

To Harold "Dutch" Haagsma, President and CEO of a California computer firm, for his review and constructive additions to the section on computers.

To Dr. Lauren Bentt, who heads the pain clinic at the Greater Southeast Hospital, Washington, D.C., for her information on the latest techniques to combat pain.

To Chaplain Ron Schneider of the Prince George's County (Maryland) Hospice for his comments about his experiences with the dying.

To Dr. Robert Washington, Dottie Ward-Wimmer, and Kevin O'Brien of the William Wendt Center for Loss and Healing, Washington, D.C., which specializes in grief counseling, for their insights on grief, death, and dying.

To nurse Ardelle Woodring of the Prince George's Hospice for sharing with us her experiences in caring for the dying.

We also want to thank the retirees in the following retirement groups for sharing with us their experiences with retirement: Moravian Manor, Lititz, Pennsylvania; Moravian Hall Square, Nazareth, Pennsylvania; Kirkland Village, Bethlehem, Pennsylvania; Kirkwood Village, Loudoun County, Virginia; and the Slightly Older Guys and Gals (SLOGGS) of Upper Marlboro, Maryland. Our sincere thanks for your participation.

Writing this book has been a joy for many reasons, not the least of which is that it has given us a meaningful project in our retirement that has allowed us to work together on something of interest and importance. It also has allowed us to come in contact with a number of fantastic people who have been willing to share their time and expertise with us (and, through this book, with you). The people named here—and many we don't have space to mention—have enriched our lives and made this book possible. To them we express our sincere gratitude.

L. James and Jackie Harvey

Contents

PREFACE

We are finding our retirement years to be the best years of our lives. We write from our experience and sincerely hope what we are discovering will help you experience the joy of what we prefer to call the *refocused* years, rather than the retirement years.

The word *retirement* always has seemed inappropriate to describe what we are experiencing. *Retired* connotes that one has stopped doing something, has withdrawn, or gone to the sidelines. But retirement is just the opposite. While it is true we both have relinquished full-time jobs, we are as active now in other—even more important—activities as we were before.

Our retirement has not meant a withdrawal or a move to the sidelines. It has meant a *refocusing* of our activity—a marvelous focusing on the things we want to do, on the things we like to do, and, we believe, on the things God wants us to do. True, we no longer work as we once did to make a living or to raise our family, but we are no less active. The difference is we are doing things that are more exciting, more fun, and no less meaningful than when we worked. In fact, in many ways, the things we are doing in retirement are more meaningful than what we did in our earlier years.

We used to be a little embarrassed when people asked if we were retired. To admit we were seemed to say we were no longer involved in meaningful everyday activity—that we were mainly resting on the sidelines of life which is the very opposite of what we are doing. So we prefer, when people ask us if we are retired, to say, "No, we are just *refocused*." That seems to convey more accurately our current status. We have refocused our energies on things we like to do and want to do. We have a new freedom to follow our interests and to do those things that are more meaningful to us than simply earning a living. It's a great time—one of the best times of our lives.

Every period of life has its pluses and minuses. Childhood is full of energy and the excitement of growing and learning. All our needs are met by others, usually our parents. However, we are dependent, we must live within the limits others impose on us, and we suffer physical and mental pain as we learn the lessons of life. There are tradeoffs—just as there are in every period of life. There are good things and bad things. Whether we are happy or unhappy depends on how we react to the realities of that stage of our development. It is no different in the *refocused* years. They can be the best years of life or the worst. It depends largely on how we deal with the pluses and minuses. In the following pages, we discuss these issues frankly, including the issue of facing our own death, which we believe must be dealt with to prosper in the *refocused* years.

We sincerely hope this book helps you find the joy and fulfillment we have found in these later years of our lives. We bring to this book the experiences from our *refocused* years as well as the experiences of a lifetime that helped prepare us for them. Jim brings a doctorate in counseling, as well as experience as an athlete, coach, counselor, educator, college administrator, management consultant, author, registered financial planner, father of four, and active church worker. Jackie brings experience as an honor student, housewife, mother of four, grandmother of eight (so far), active church worker, longtime employee in a correctional facility, and trained volunteer for a county hospice program. Her work with the dying made a critical contribution to the chapter on death, perhaps the most important chapter in the book.

It is our prayer that God will use this book to help you find every ounce of joy and meaning you can from your *refocusment*. We hope you also embrace the attitude that during *refocusment*, every day is Saturday.

Introduction

TEN COMMANDMENTS FOR RETIREMENT

Enjoy and appreciate old age—
many people never have the privilege

When we were kids, Saturday was the greatest day of the week. It was the day when Dad was home, the day the family went places and did things together. It was the day we didn't have to get up early to go to school. As we grew up, Saturday was the day we went on dates, went on hayrides, and went to athletic events. Saturday was the day we looked forward to all week because it was the day we could do what we most wanted to do.

When we were searching for a title for this book, it dawned on us that retirement is a lot like Saturdays were for us as kids. Retirement is when we can do the things we most want to do. We are no longer bound by a workweek where our efforts are prescribed by others. We have gained a freedom to do those things we most want to do. In retirement, every day is indeed Saturday. It's fantastic!

Don't get us wrong. Sunday is still the most important day. It is the day we go to God's house, worship Him, listen to His Word, dine at His Table, fellowship with our brothers and sisters in Christ, and recharge our spiritual batteries. Sunday is special for these reasons. But every other day is Saturday.

Retirement, like most everything else in life, is what you make of it. It can be viewed pessimistically as the period in life when your physical and mental capabilities slowly degenerate until death relieves you of your pain. Or it can be viewed as a fantastic period of opportunity, joy, peace, and service until your joyful homecoming with the Lord. The choice is really yours. And we have more capacity to make this choice than you might think. Dr. Ben Carson, one of America's leading neurosurgeons at Johns Hopkins University in Baltimore, tells us that "this divinely created brain has 14 billion cells. If used to the maximum, this human computer inside our heads could contain all the knowledge from the beginning of the world to the present and still have room left over."[1]

In a speech before a group in our county, Carson said that if we were to try to replicate the human brain in a modern computer, we would have to build one that is 60 stories high and covers the same area as the city of Dallas. Isn't that amazing? And God has given each one of us a free "computer." But wait. It gets even better. Through research, we know our wonderful computers don't wear out as we age. Carson indicates we can learn unlimited amounts of new things until the day we die. Our brains slow down a bit and short-term memory may get sluggish, but our basic capacity to learn and remember is retained throughout life, as long as we use our brains and they are free of disease.

With some education and effort, we can use our "computers" to our benefit and make retirement the best years of our lives.

Positive Thinking

Most bookstores have shelves full of books written by psychologists and others trying to convince people that if they think positively they will be better off. These writers are making millions because positive thinking works; in fact, it is a biblically based concept.

> And we know that in *all* things God works for the good of those who love Him, who have been called according to His purpose. (Romans 8:28, emphasis added)

God has called us and made us His own through Jesus' saving work on the cross. And He promises to work in *everything* for our good. You can't get more positive than that.

There is something to be said for attitude. We determine whether our retirement is good or bad, happy or sad, productive or nonproductive, joyous or depressing. We choose! And Romans 8:28 reminds us that God is right there with us. Even through the difficult and painful experiences, He promises to work through them for our good. With that kind of promise, with the love and forgiveness of Jesus Christ, with the Holy Spirit working in our lives, with God's guardian angels watching over us, with the brainpower God has given us to choose a positive attitude, why would retirement be anything but the best time of our lives?

Meaning in Life

It's been said that life without meaning is not worth living and lack of meaning may even lead to death. In his book *Man's Search for Meaning*, eminent Austrian psychiatrist Viktor Frankl describes his own life, particularly his experiences in four concentration camps during World War II. Frankl was interested in finding out why some people died and others survived in these camps made infamous by Hitler's Holocaust. Frankl concluded that those who lived had something to live for. They had goals or loved ones or faith that gave meaning to life. Those who had no meaning died.

An even more dramatic demonstration of this truth occurred during the Korean War. The American government became concerned when they found that American prisoners were giving up hope and dying in the prisoner of war camps. No prisoners were escaping as they had in every other war in history. The government learned that the Chinese Communists had instituted a sophisticated brainwashing technique based on psychological principles.

James Stokesbury describes these brainwashing techniques (sometimes called re-education) and their success in his book *A Short History of the Korean War*. He reports that 38 percent of the American prisoners of war died in the prison camps of Korea compared to a death rate of only 4 percent in the German POW camps of World War II. Stokesbury also tells about the large number of POWs who made radio broadcasts for the Communists that were critical of the United States. The American government began a study to determine what was happening to these prisoners that had not occurred in previous wars. The study continued after the war and the remaining POWs came home.

The study found that the Chinese attempted to cut the ties of American POWs to everything that was meaningful to them so they could build new ties to Communism and to the Chinese instead. The Chinese let "Dear John letters" get through to the prisoners but not letters with positive news from back home. They filled the prisoners' minds with lies about America and about the war. They forced them to be indoctrinated into Communist ideology. When the positive ties to home, family, and country were broken, some men refused to build ties to the enemy. They literally lay down and died. The condition was labeled "give-up-itis." Other POWs found if they couldn't get the person on his feet within 24 hours, even by hitting him or making him mad, he would die. The destruction of all meaningful ties led to death.

Some prisoners never lost faith or meaning, and they survived. Others succumbed to Chinese propaganda and became traitors, staying in China even after the war ended. Still others, like the Turks, had such strong national and military ties that not one prisoner died or was brainwashed. As a result of the study, the U.S. military made significant changes in its training of troops to help them better handle brainwashing.

While we're not saying retirees are "prisoners" by any means, there is some correlation. Consider the man who builds his whole life around his wife. He derives all meaning in life from her. Then she dies. He dies soon after because his life has lost all meaning. Or consider the woman who has built her life around her work. She has obtained nearly all her recognition and psychological rewards from her work. When work ends and retirement begins, her main support systems end and, unless there is something to replace them, she will give up and die. Before you shrug off this phenomenon, saying, "that doesn't *really* happen," stop and think. Do you know someone who retired, vegetated, and died within a year or two? It's terribly sad and also unnecessary.

So what's the lesson for retirees? To stay healthy there must be meaning to life. For the Christian, that's a cakewalk. Jesus Christ gave us "meaning" when He died to save us from our sins. Through our faith in Him and through contact with our brothers and sisters in Christ, we are reminded of that gift every day. We believe that as long as God gives us breath, He has something for us to do. Finding what that is and doing it provide the meaning we need. (We'll discuss this more in later chapters.)

But we also must have a realistic view of retirement. The book *Successful Aging* reports the results of the decade-long

MacArthur Foundation's Study of Aging in America. In chapter 1, authors John W. Rowe and Robert L. Kahn list six myths about aging.

> *Myth 1: To be old is to be sick.*
>
> *Myth 2: You can't teach an old dog new tricks.*
>
> *Myth 3: The horse is out of the barn.*
>
> *Myth 4: The secret to successful aging is to choose your parents wisely.*
>
> *Myth 5: The lights may be on but the voltage is low.*
>
> *Myth 6: The elderly don't pull their own weight.[2]*

Research shows that most seniors are not sick and the vast majority—about 95 percent—do not wind up in nursing homes. Further, we can learn until the day we die. It is a myth that positive changes in health habits cannot help us because "the damage is already done." Exercising, eating well, and quitting smoking can make a big difference, even in our senior years. Research also confirms that passion and love can continue and brighten life to the very end. Finally, research determined that seniors more than pull their own weight in society through volunteer work, part-time work, and other—often not counted—work they do for their families, neighbors, and friends. So research blows away some of the most pervasive myths and shows us instead that the "golden years" can be some of the most productive, joyful, passion-filled, healthy years of our lives, if we make the right choices.

As Billy Graham put it:

> I admit I don't like the burdens of old age—the slow decline in energy, the physical annoyances, the pain of losing loved ones, the sadness of seeing friends decline. But old age can be a special time of life, and God has lessons to teach us through it.[3]

Retirement can be a "special time" indeed. While writing this book, we developed "The Harveys' 10 Commandments for a Successful Retirement." We are convinced that following them can help you thrive and prosper in your "golden years."

The Harveys' 10 Commandments for a Successful Retirement

I. **Be active.** Mind, body, and spirit are meant to be used. Like muscles, they grow and expand when used and waste away when not used. God has given us the capacity to grow. The more you use your God-given mind, body, and spirit, the happier you will be. Positive activity promotes growth; inactivity kills.

II. **Exercise regularly.** The body slows down and atrophies when it is not used. Doctors agree that regular exercise promotes both mental and physical health. Three 20-minute exercise periods per week is a small investment of time but yields a dividend of good mental and physical health.

III. **Live your faith.** You can speak to your heavenly Father every day and hear what His words are for you—words of love and mercy through Jesus Christ. Get a good daily devotional book and use it along with your favorite study Bible to stay in touch with your Father. Attend worship services regularly. Dine often at the Lord's Table. God will strengthen your faith through His Word and Sacrament.

IV. **Help others.** The joy and satisfaction you get from helping others is great medicine for your soul. Retirement is a time to give something back to your community and to invest time in volunteer activities. You will find you get more than you give and you can't "out-give" your loving and generous heavenly Father.

V. **Control your weight.** Excess weight saps energy, corrodes your feelings about yourself, and overtaxes a number of body systems. A little discipline in this area goes a long way toward increasing the enjoyment of retirement.

VI. **Have annual physicals.** Most serious health problems can be detected during annual physical exams. Nearly all of them that are detected early can be overcome. There is no better insurance for good health than regular physical exams.

VII. **Avoid accidents.** Accidents that would simply harm a younger person can debilitate or even kill a senior citizen. Pay attention to the key principles listed in chapter 2 to help you avoid dangerous situations.

VIII. **Be computer literate.** In the Information Age, no device opens the world of knowledge the way the computer does. Don't be afraid—computers can be easy to use and can add meaning and joy to your life.

IX. **Enjoy humor and good music.** There is a reason comedians and musicians have longer life spans than people in other occupations. Laughter and good music are like medicine to the body and spirit. The writer of Proverbs even tells us, "A cheerful heart is good medicine" (Proverbs 17:22). Good humor and good music produce a sense of joy and well being that makes for good health.

X. Obey God's Ten Commandments. As redeemed children of God, we know that He gave us the Ten Commandments to show us our sins but also to guide us by His grace in living a productive, Christ-centered, joy-filled life. They apply as much in the golden years as in childhood. Ask God's help to follow His commands.

Major Issues

The rest of the chapters in this book focus on issues critical to the retiree. These issues are presented here as elements of a cross to help you remember them.

First, we will cover the subject of faith because it is central to all the other issues of retirement. Following the discussion of faith, we will cover health, activity, finance, and, finally, death. Within this framework, we will present the knowledge and information we believe you need to have a joyous retirement.

Throughout the book, you will find humor because we

"You don't look anything like the long haired, skinny kid I married 25 years ago. I need a DNA sample to make sure it's still you."

believe God intended for us to have a merry heart and because it is good for us. In chapter 3, we have included a section on computers because we are in the Information Age and the computer is a tool that unlocks an entire new world to the retiree. (And computers aren't going away anytime soon, so you may as well embrace them!) Along the way and in the appendices, we have included as much information and related references as we could find to help make the best of your retirement so you can join with us in proclaiming that every day is Saturday.

You can't get eyestrain from looking on the bright side of things.

FAITH

The Core of a Successful Retirement

Faith

The Christian life consists in faith and charity. — *Martin Luther*

For it is by grace you have been saved, through faith—and
this not from yourselves, it is the gift of God—not by works,
so that no one can boast. (Ephesians 2:8–9)

No element of a Christian's life is more important than
faith. We have put it at the center of the cross on the opposite
page because faith is central to everything in life—including
retirement. Without faith in Christ Jesus, the "golden years"
will have no glitter at all. Without faith, the "golden years" will
be, at best, "fool's gold."

One of the best things about retirement is that we can
enjoy faith more fully and continue to grow in that faith. We
can spend more time with the Lord through study of His Word
and in prayer, and we can ask Him to continue to deepen and
enrich our faith. An ever-maturing faith holds the key to joy in
retirement and to preparation for the fantastic life to come
when, as we discuss in chapter 5, we are "transferred to the
home office."

One of the great blessings of a mature faith is a "peace at the center." This, too, comes as a gift from God, as St. Paul says:

> Therefore, since we have been justified through faith, we have peace with God through our Lord Jesus Christ, through whom we have gained access by faith into this grace in which we now stand. And we rejoice in the hope of the glory of God. (Romans 5:1–2)

Did you get that promise? We receive peace and joy from our faith and can look forward to sharing in the glory of God when we go to heaven. You have to *work* to be sad with promises like this.

Paul also records a prayer we can say for ourselves and other believers:

> I pray that out of His glorious riches He may strengthen you with power through His Spirit in your inner being, so that Christ may dwell in your hearts through faith. And I pray that you, being rooted and established in love, may have power, together with all the saints, to grasp how wide and long and high and deep is the love of Christ, and to know this love that surpasses knowledge—that you may be filled to the measure of all the fullness of God. (Ephesians 3:16–19)

Wow! What a wonderful prayer—and promise! Because Christ lives in our hearts through faith and we are grounded in His love, we will have wisdom that is unsurpassed, we will know the love of Christ, and we will experience the fullness of God. How good can it get?

God fills us to overflowing out of His own fullness. He gives us faith, love for Him and our fellow man, and the Holy

Spirit to comfort us and to guide us. God's fullness includes in abundant measure "the peace that passes understanding" and a "joy unspeakable." God knows how to give good gifts.

Sorrow looks back, worry looks around, faith looks up.

The faithful Christian looks up. Sorrow and worry are not the Christian's lot and need not diminish our retirement years. We have God's faithful promises of salvation and eternal life in Christ Jesus, which give us hope despite our physical or financial circumstances. Most of us can think of some saintly Christian whose face literally glowed with peace and joy. The sparkling eye, the smile-wrinkled face, the sense of humor, and the peace with life are the trademarks of the elderly Christian. Contrast this with the grouchy, frowning, sad face of the elderly curmudgeon and you get a clear picture of the difference faith can make.

*He who has the faith has the fun.
—G.K. Chesterton*

G.K. Chesterton, the early 20th-century English essayist and humorist, has it right. The faithful have the fun—fun in the sense of depth of peace and joy, not a superficial fun that masks depression and hurt. A real sense of humor and joy that laughs *with* people and not *at* them is a by-product of faith.

We are not called to be successful, but to be faithful. —Mother Teresa

Mother Teresa knew faith in Christ was the key to life here and in heaven. The world measures success in terms of money and possessions, but God looks at us through the cross of

Christ. He sees us as His beloved children, redeemed by the blood of His Son. God loves us, and His merciful love frees us to share our faith with others as we lovingly serve them in His name.

> "Do not store up for yourselves treasures on earth, where moth and rust destroy, and where thieves break in and steal. But store up for yourselves treasures in heaven, where moth and rust do not destroy, and where thieves do not break in and steal. For where your treasure is, there your heart will be also." (Matthew 6:19–21)

God has given each of us numerous treasures—gifts to use in service to others. Especially in retirement, you have daily opportunities to employ these gifts. Ask the Holy Spirit to help you live your faith as He guides you to serve others. As Jesus said,

> "The King will reply, 'I tell you the truth, whatever you did for one of the least of these brothers of Mine, you did for Me.'" (Matthew 25:40)

When you help those in need—the poor, those in prison, those God puts in front of you—you demonstrate living faith. If you find yourself praying for others, volunteering to help others, giving to spread the Gospel, and looking for opportunities to serve God and others, your faith is alive. As the apostle James says:

> I will show you my faith by what I do. (James 2:18)

But can retirees continue to grow in faith? Yes! Faith, like our bodies and minds, grows with use.

> For this very reason, make every effort to add to your faith

goodness; and to goodness, knowledge; and to knowledge, self-control; and to self-control, perseverance; and to perseverance, godliness; and to godliness, brotherly kindness; and to brotherly kindness, love. For if you possess these qualities in increasing measure, they will keep you from being ineffective and unproductive in your knowledge of our Lord Jesus Christ. (2 Peter 1:5–8)

How do retirees grow in faith? By attending worship, by studying God's Word, by partaking of His Holy Meal, by conversing with Him in prayer, by learning more about Him, by doing His work, and by socializing with mature brothers and sisters in Christ.

As we've said, one of retirement's blessings is that we can reprogram our time to do the "more important" things. It's easier now to make time for daily devotions, to join a weekly or daily Bible study group, and to volunteer at church or with community organizations. As we spend time with God in His Word and Sacrament, His Holy Spirit will continue to grow and strengthen our faith, even in our retirement years!

The apostle Paul never retired, nor should we. Refocus, yes; retire, no. Our "refocusment" years allow us new opportunities to ask the Holy Spirit to strengthen our faith and to live it out in daily life. As we continue to grow in God's grace, we will reap peace and joy as we prepare for our glorious homecoming. How good can it get?

I have fought the good fight, I have finished the race, I have kept the faith. Now there is in store for me the crown of righteousness, which the Lord, the righteous Judge, will award to me on that day—and not only to me, but also to all who have longed for His appearing. (2 Timothy 4:7–8)

two

HEALTH

From Major Senior Maladies to Healthy Living

Hardening of the heart—not the arteries—makes one old.

The LORD gives strength to His people; the LORD blesses His people with peace. (Psalm 29:11)

Next to our faith, nothing is more important to our well being in the golden years than our health. And we can do much to ensure we remain healthy as medical science continues to do more to overcome disease, illness, and pain. In their book *Successful Aging,* John Rowe and Robert Kahn cite significant data to dispel the myth that the senior years are filled with illness and disability. The vast majority of golden-agers can live healthy, productive lives if they make the right choices.

Nearly every day brings news of a new drug or a breakthrough in research that promises to attack a dreaded disease on a new front. Those of us over 60 can remember easily when tuberculosis and polio were feared diseases that crippled and killed millions. These diseases are no longer the threats they once were, and we are on the verge of eliminating polio from the world forever. We now have hope that in our lifetime most cancers, too, will be defeated as new treatments and drugs are being discovered and announced frequently.

One of the great fears of older adults is pain and the conditions surrounding the approach of death. There is great news here also because science and the medical profession are making marvelous progress in treating pain. Even as this book is being written, news reports tell of a new painkilling drug that is many times stronger and more effective than morphine, the strongest painkiller we have at present.

This chapter will present information on the essentials of good health and how to avoid and conquer the major health problems seniors face. At the end of the chapter, there are sections for "Him" and for "Her" that focus on gender-related health issues. So be of good cheer—healthy living is attainable, even if you're just starting now.

Accidents

Recent information from the National Center for Injury Prevention and Control's website (**www.cdc.gov/ncipc**)[4] indicates:

- One of every three seniors over 65 falls each year.

- Of those who fall, 20–30 percent will suffer moderate to severe injuries causing reduced mobility and independence and a greater risk of death.

- The direct medical costs of fall-related injuries run in the billions of dollars each year.

- The economic impact of osteoporosis (brittle bone disease) fractures is estimated to exceed $45.2 billion in the year 2000.

- Hip fractures are the most serious for seniors and lead to the greatest number of health problems and deaths.

If you want to keep a good quality of life and avoid premature death, you can take extra measures to avoid accidents. Research provides us with a wealth of material to aid us in avoiding accidents and falls. Following is some of the more salient information to help you avoid accident-related problems.

Protecting against Accidents

1. **Exercise regularly.** You've heard it said a million times, but it's true: Regular exercise is perhaps the most beneficial thing you can do to extend and preserve the quality of life. Exercise strengthens both bones and muscles, helping seniors avoid falls through better balance and the capability to "catch yourself" before falling. Exercise also minimizes the damage from a fall, should one occur, and promotes faster healing should damage occur. A regular exercise program, coupled with a balanced diet and vitamin supplements, can be your most effective insurance policy against accidents.

2. **Practice safety at home.** Most falls occur at home. Study your home to find and eliminate possible causes of falls. Study your floors and steps to make sure there are no protrusions on which you might catch your foot. Use stepladders with great caution. Make sure they are stable, set up properly, and in good repair. In winter, use extra caution on snow and ice. When you reach the older years (75+), you may want to move to a ranch home with the major living space on one floor. You also may consider moving to a warmer climate, at least in the winter, to avoid ice and snow.

3. **Practice safety when driving.**

   a.) Wear seat belts at all times.

   b.) If you drink, let someone else drive.

   c.) Plan trips during the middle of the day when traffic is lighter.

   d.) Do not drive when you are drowsy. Falling asleep at the wheel is the greatest single cause of accidents on the nation's freeways. If you feel drowsy, stop and take a nap or allow someone else to drive. Sleep sneaks up on you before you know it. Drive defensively, and be aware that someone else on the road may endanger you.

   e.) Remember that the single greatest cause of auto accidents for seniors is making left turns across a flow of traffic. As we age, our eyes and ability to perceive and process information slow somewhat; therefore, we are more prone than younger drivers to misjudge the speed of oncoming traffic. While your perception problem may be slight, it can lead to an accident. Plan trips so you can get where you are going without left turns across major lanes of traffic, and be extra cautious whenever you must make a left turn.

   f.) Avoid nighttime driving if possible. As we age, our night vision is not as good as when we were younger. Our ability to see other traffic and judge speeds is lessened, so nighttime driving becomes more dangerous. This is particularly true for those 75 years old or older. If you must drive at night, be extra careful.

National Institute on Aging (NIA) Recommendations

The NIA lists the following things you should do if you want to live a healthy life and avoid serious health problems in retirement.

1. Eat a balanced diet, including five helpings of fruits and vegetables each day.

2. Exercise regularly.

3. Get regular health checkups.

4. Don't smoke.

5. Practice safety habits at home to prevent falls and fractures. Always wear a seat belt in the car.

GLASBERGEN

"Thank you for calling the Weight Loss Hotline. If you'd like to lose 1/2 pound right now, press 1 eighteen thousand times."

© 1997 RANDY GLASBERGEN

6. Stay in contact with family and friends. Stay active through work, play, and community.

7. Avoid overexposure to sun and cold.

8. If you drink, moderation is the key. When you drink, let someone else drive.

9. Keep personal and financial records in order to simplify budgeting and investing. Plan long-term housing and money needs.

10. Keep a positive attitude toward life. Do things that make you happy.[5]

All of that is good advice, but it lacks the most important element: God. We prefer to add a number 11 to the list:

11. Live your faith. Study God's Word, worship often, dine with the Lord frequently, pray,

enjoy regular fellowship with your brothers and sisters in Christ, and ask the Holy Spirit to guide you in new ways to live your faith by sharing God's love with others.

Healthy Living

Let's take a closer look at some of the points from the NIA's list.

Exercise Regularly

You'll notice this one keeps popping up. That's because it's important! Regular exercise means at least three 20-minute periods a week of aerobic activity—something that raises the heart rate and increases the supply of oxygen to the body. Brisk walking is good exercise, as are swimming, aerobic exercise classes, dancing, etc. (Always check with your doctor before beginning a new program.) Research shows that you can add muscle mass through weightlifting even in your 90s.

Exercise improves balance (which helps you avoid falls) and improves circulation, as well as heart and lung function, helping the body nourish itself and defend against disease.

Exercise *can* be fun and, with a little planning, it can be something you'll look forward to. Most senior centers have senior exercise programs. Every major city has exercise clubs and facilities you can join. Many large shopping malls have walking clubs where you can socialize and walk with others.

If you prefer, you can buy exercise equipment for home use. A plethora of new equipment hits the market on a regular basis. Beware of false claims made by the manufacturers, however. Do not buy equipment unless you try it out first and are certain you will maintain a program if you buy it. Don't buy exercise equipment advertised in TV infomercials that you can't get in a store. Most items don't live up to their TV promises and can be more difficult to return than you'd think. And don't buy something that promises to get you in shape "in just four weeks at four minutes a day!" Nothing works that fast. So shop around. You may find great deals on exercise equipment at yard sales because people are selling products they bought with good intentions they didn't follow through on.

If you buy exercise equipment, make sure you get equipment that will allow you to work all the major muscle groups, including your arms and upper body, your abdominal and back muscles, and your legs and lower body muscles. A good workout three times a week can do wonders for the body, mind, and spirit.

If you exercise alone, you may want to listen to the radio or watch TV while you work out. Such a distraction makes the time seem to pass faster and combines exercise with entertainment—a combination that's hard to beat.

Stop Bad Habits

Smoking, excessive drinking, and overeating are the three most common causes of senior health problems. The good news is, no matter how old you are or how long you have followed a bad habit, you will benefit from stopping it. God has given the human body a remarkable ability to repair itself if we stop abusing it and instead care for it properly.

Many seniors tend to become sedentary upon retirement. That is the opposite of what the body needs. God created the human body to be used. Like any good piece of machinery, it has built-in systems to keep it running and in good condition. The body needs clean air and oxygen, healthy food, and clean water to function properly. If it gets these things, as well as moderate exercise, it will work wonderfully.

The body also has built-in defenses against illness and disease. A healthy immune system will help keep us disease-free if we use reasonable judgment about how we live. A doctor once told us that the body is naturally inclined toward health. Problems generally develop only when bad habits or outside factors interfere with the natural momentum toward good health.

Maintain a Reasonable Weight

We've all heard the alarming statistics about the increasing number of Americans who are, by definition, obese. You even may have seen a report on a TV news program about airlines, bus and car manufacturers, and office chair manufacturers changing industry standards for the width of the average chair. Such an increase in the standard width is necessary because so many Americans are overweight.

As we age and retire, we may become slightly less active, which means our bodies need fewer calories. If we do not compensate by eating less, we will add extra, unwanted, pounds. It's that simple.

> Do not join with those who drink too much wine or gorge themselves on meat, for drunkards and gluttons become poor, and drowsiness clothes them in rags. (Proverbs 23:20–21)

Being overweight has severe health ramifications. Based on new research, the American Heart Association has, for the first time, added obesity to its list of "major risk" factors for heart disease. Obesity joins these other factors on the list: smoking, high blood pressure, high cholesterol, and a sedentary lifestyle.

How do you know if you're obese? In 1995, the U.S. National Institutes of Health (NIH) and the American Health Foundation released a standard for determining obesity called the Body Mass Index (BMI). In 1998, they modified the standards somewhat. You can determine where you fall on the scale from underweight to gross obesity by calculating your BMI:

$$BMI = \frac{703 \times \text{(your weight in pounds)}}{\text{(your height in inches)}^2}$$

For example, if a person weighs 175 pounds and is 5-feet 11-inches tall (that's 71 inches), the calculation is as follows:

$$BMI = \frac{703 \times 175}{71^2}$$

Or

$$123,025 \div 5041 = 24.4$$

So if you weigh 175 pounds and are 5-feet 11-inches tall, your BMI is 24.4. But what does that mean? The following table shows the BMI scale from underweight to gross obesity. The standards are the same for men and women. Calculate your own BMI and find the number on the table below. Note that research currently indicates health risks develop gradually, starting in people with a BMI of 25 and becoming more serious as the BMI increases.

Body Mass Index

0–18.5	Underweight
18.6–25	Normal weight range
25–30	Overweight (health risks begin to increase)
30–40	Obese (definite health risks occur)
40+	Gross obesity (serious health risks)

Current medical research also says it is *more* unhealthy to lose weight, gain it back, and lose it again, engaging in what is called the "yo-yo effect." If you are serious about losing weight, make the lifestyle changes to keep it off or the weight will come right back and your body will be negatively affected by the changes. You are better off health-wise to stay overweight (not obese) than to lose and gain in a yo-yo pattern. The only effective way to lose and keep weight off is to change what you eat (reduce calories, particularly from fats) and increase your exercise (burn more calories).

Even if you don't have a serious weight problem, you'll be better off if you make a concerted effort to do two things:

1. Never put food in your mouth until the previous mouthful has been thoroughly chewed and swallowed.

2. Chew your food twice as long as you have in the past. You will double your pleasure from eating while making things easier for your digestive tract. Most seniors could cut their food consumption in half by chewing twice as long. You'll end up enjoying eating as much as you always have while consuming half the calories. Try it—you'll like it.

According to many people who reduced their weight from overweight to normal range, one of the greatest benefits of maintaining a proper weight is an increased energy level. Many report both physical and psychological benefits from weight loss that gives life a new vitality and excitement.

Avoid Overexposure to the Sun

Aging skin is vulnerable to skin cancer caused by overexposure to the sun. With age, skin pigment declines, and the ultraviolet rays penetrate more easily, causing damage and promoting pre-cancerous and cancerous growths. If you are going to be in the sun for any length of time, use a sunscreen with a Sun Protective Factor (SPF) of at least 15. If you notice any changes in your skin (discoloration, bumps, scaly growths, etc.), talk to your doctor about them. Most common skin cancers can be treated if caught early.

Have Annual Physical Exams

Most health problems can be cured or contained if detected early. The annual physical for the senior becomes one of the best guarantees of a happy, healthy retirement. Women should have an annual Pap smear and a mammogram. Men should have a PSA test at least every 12 months to check for prostate cancer. Talk to your doctor about your family's health history. He or she may require other annual tests for you if you are at risk for high blood pressure, stroke, heart attack, or other serious illnesses.

Eat a Balanced Diet and Take a Vitamin Supplement

Eating a balanced diet, including fresh fruit, is an insurance policy for good health. Health experts also recommend a vitamin supplement, particularly one that contains antioxidants: vitamin C, vitamin E, and beta-carotene. Some companies make multivitamin supplements just for seniors. Be advised, however, that the research on the value of vitamin supplements is not definitive. As with dieting and exercise, talk to your doctor before you take vitamin supplements. He or she can recommend what is best for your individual needs.

Laugh and Listen to Good Music

Ever notice that musicians and comedians seem to live longer than people in other professions? In 1976, author Norman Cousins brought national attention to the subject of

**After two weeks of dieting,
Larry's fat cells decided to go out for a pizza.**

GLASBERGEN

© 1996 RANDY GLASBERGEN.

humor and health when he wrote that he had laughed his way to recovery from a degenerative spinal condition. That led to a national symposium on humor in 1982 and the publication of papers presented at the symposium in *Handbook of Humor Research.*

In 1988, the American Association for Therapeutic Humor (AATH) was founded. Research indicates that laughter reduces stress, strengthens the immune system, and leads to a healthy sense of well-being. In short, reports the AATH, "Happy people live longer."

Put on a smile, sing a hymn, and watch your troubles flee.

A similar finding has come in the field of music. The American Music Therapy Association (AMTA) researches the healing properties of music and promotes the training of music therapists who facilitate healing using music. If you would like to visit the organization's website and learn more, you will find it at **www.musictherapy.com**. The association also publishes a scientific journal, *The Journal of Music Therapy.*

Another professional association dealing with these issues is the Associates for Research Into the Science of Enjoyment (ARISE). This is an international organization based in England that promotes research on the effects of enjoyment on humans and their health. The group's website is **www.arise.org**.

So to review: Music and laughter make us feel good. They relieve stress and leave us with a sense of well-being. Science says they're good for us. So build them into your daily activities. If you do, the research says you will live a longer and happier life.

How do you add music and laughter to your routine? For starters, invest in good stereo systems for your home and car—you're investing in your health. When you get in your car, turn on some great music and relax. Listen to the music and think about how it makes you feel. Don't listen to music that makes you uptight and tense; listen to something that makes you relax (but not so much that it puts you to sleep!). We take a host of great Christian artists wherever we go.

Music is the gift of God—I place it next to theology. —*Martin Luther*

Adding music is easy. What about laughter? We are more psychologically healthy when we learn to laugh at ourselves. A healthier attitude about ourselves makes us easier to live with. If you don't have a great sense of humor, you can develop one by paying attention to the humor around you. Read jokes and cartoons and pass them on to others. (We've included a handful of jokes in Appendix E to get you started.) Find good books on humor and share them with others. You might enjoy *Let There Be Laughter* by Rich and Bob Bimler (Concordia, 1999), which is all about adding "holy hilarity" to your life. Or you may want to become a member of the Fellowship of Merry Christians. This group offers a humor newsletter and other ways to celebrate the life that is ours in Christ. Find out more about this organization at **www.joyfulnoiseletter.com**. This website suggests a number of books on living joyfully.

So if you want to improve your health and increase your enjoyment of life, laugh, sing, and surround yourself with great music whenever you can.

Avoid Stress

Stress and tension can negatively affect your health. But can you avoid stress altogether? A friend of ours told us that when he retired, he was going to list the things that caused him the most stress and he was going to avoid them. Seem too simple? Maybe, but there is some truth here.

"My doctor keeps telling me I need to relax... but relaxation makes me tense!"

List the top three things that cause you stress. Then develop a plan of attack for either reducing or eliminating the stress and tension caused by these things. (Warning: If your spouse turns out to be one of the three, you'd better have a serious talk or head for marital counseling.) Once you've taken care of your first list, make another. Systematically reduce the stress and tension in your life. For example, if traffic stresses you, try to drive when there is less traffic, or give yourself more time for the trips you must make. If you know it will take you 25 minutes to drive to the doctor, give yourself 45 minutes to arrive. Then when you get stuck behind that slow driver or lodged in a traffic jam, you won't be stressed because you'll still have plenty of time to reach your destination. By paying attention to what causes you stress and working to eliminate those situations, you will live a happier, more product life in your refocused years.

Major Senior Maladies

You may have noticed that this chapter's subtitle is *From Major Senior Maladies to Healthy Living.* Why did we talk about the healthy living first? Because it's the focus of this chapter and should be a focus in your retirement. But knowing and understanding the major health threats to seniors can help you avoid or minimize their impact. The rest of this chapter will discuss the major problems many seniors face.

Cancer

Cancer is the uncontrolled growth of abnormal cells, which, if unchecked, can choke off normal functions and lead to death. Many types of cancer are now treatable, particularly if caught early. Prevention and early detection are the chief ways to fight cancer. Some of the most common cancers are

1. **Breast cancer**—(See "Just for Her" for further details.)

2. **Prostate cancer**—(See "Just for Him" for further details.)

3. **Pelvic and cervical cancer**—(See "Just for Her" for further details.)

4. **Colorectal cancer**—Early detection is the primary way to fight this cancer. As part of an annual physical, seniors should have a rectal exam and a blood stool test. Every three to four years, you should have an examination of the rectum and lower colon using an instrument called a sigmoidoscope. Medicare covers colorectal screening tests that could save your life. If (between annual physicals) you detect any bleeding when eliminating, contact your doctor at once. It may be nothing serious, but if it is, early detection can save your life.

5. **Lung cancer**—Smoking causes lung cancer. If you don't smoke, your chances of getting lung cancer are reduced significantly. If you live in an environment where someone else smokes (exposing you to secondary smoke), your chances of getting lung cancer are increased significantly. Helping a spouse or close relative with whom you live stop smoking may save

his or her life as well as your own. As of this writing, there are no good screening tests for lung cancer. If you have a cough that will not go away or shortness of breath unrelated to exercise or a specific incident, talk to your doctor right away.

6. **Skin cancer**—The most common form of skin cancer, basal cell cancer, is easily detected and easily treated. Most skin cancer is a result of overexposure to the ultraviolet rays of the sun. Avoiding overexposure and using sunscreen with an SPF of at least 15 will help prevent skin cancer. If you notice anything different about your skin, such as discoloration, bumps, scaly areas, or moles that change shape or color, talk to your doctor about it.

Heart Disease

After age 60, heart disease is the primary killer of both men and women, killing one in four. Smoking, high blood pressure, and high cholesterol are major causes of heart disease. Exercise and regular blood pressure and cholesterol checks can help prevent the problem. From angioplasty to heart bypass operations to heart transplants, medicine has come a long way in treating heart problems. However, prevention is far better than treatment.

"Gravity has lowered my chest, my stomach and my butt—why hasn't it lowered my cholesterol?"

The Framingham Study, which has been in progress for more than 40 years, continues to provide significant research on heart disease, its causes, and ways to prevent it. Thousands of men and women have been followed to study the effects of various lifestyles and behavior patterns on heart health. Reports and updates of the study can be found on the National Institutes of Health website at **www.nih.gov**.

The Framingham Study confirms much of what we already know about heart disease but gives additional information as well.

- Smoking causes heart disease.

- High blood pressure is not a normal consequence of aging.

- High cholesterol leads to heart disease.

- Diabetes is a risk factor in heart disease.

- Women are at risk for heart disease but at a point later in life than men.

- One's weight affects blood pressure, and eating too much saturated fat raises cholesterol levels.

- Age and smoking compound the ill effects of the other risk factors.

- Menopause and the loss of natural estrogen increase the risk of heart disease for women. Estrogen replacement therapy can reduce this risk.

- High levels of the good cholesterol—high-density lipoprotein (HDL)—actually protect against heart disease.

- Fluctuations in weight (yo-yo dieting, which is discussed earlier in this chapter) poses a heart risk.

The Framingham Study also reports that lifestyle is more important than genetics in determining the risk for heart disease. Statistics show Americans are becoming more obese and more sedentary—just the opposite of what we should do to combat heart disease. The experts say that to be healthy, you need to eat sensibly; exercise regularly; monitor your blood pressure and cholesterol levels; not smoke; if you drink, do so moderately; keep your weight within acceptable levels; and monitor other risk factors mentioned above. Heart disease is preventable.

Stroke

Strokes are the result of coronary artery disease. They result from a blockage, usually a clot, in an artery that deprives the brain of oxygen. After a short time, this deprivation will lead to the death of brain cells and the loss of the bodily functions these cells control. In some situations, this loss of function results in paralysis. The symptoms of a stroke are

1. Sudden numbness, weakness, or paralysis of the face, arm, or leg, especially on one side of the body.

2. Sudden confusion or trouble talking or understanding others.

3. An abrupt change in vision that causes difficulty seeing in one or both eyes.

4. Sudden trouble walking or loss of balance or coordination.

It is critical to get treatment as soon as possible after a stroke. A new anti-clot drug called tissue plasminogen activator (TPA) can break up clots, restore the blood flow, and prevent paralysis. But the drug must be administered within three hours of the stroke to be effective.

Because the causes of a stroke are similar to the causes of heart disease, prevention is much the same.

Alzheimer's Disease

Alzheimer's disease has a genetic component—if family members have had the disease, your chances of getting it increase. Alzheimer's afflicts an estimated 4 million Americans. Its main symptom is progressive memory loss, but it also can cause difficulties with vision, language, and emotional control. Recent research done at Case Western Reserve University indicates that regular exercise may lower the risk for Alzheimer's disease. Currently, two drugs are approved for the treatment of Alzheimer's—Cognex and Aricept. Neither drug cures the disease; rather, they slow the degenerative process. Research continues on a number of drugs that hold promise for more effective treatment.

Rheumatoid Arthritis

This category of ailments affects the muscles, cartilage, and membranes of joints, causing stiffness, pain, redness, and tenderness in the joints. Severe types of arthritis can cause deformities and crippling. The disease affects women three times more than men and peaks from ages 35 to 45. Marvelous advancements have been made in surgical procedures and joint replacements, so even severe, crippling forms of the disease can be treated successfully. For less severe cases, new pain medications significantly improve quality of life for those suffering from arthritis. It is estimated that 75 percent of people with the disease can be treated successfully and become symptom free within one year.

High Blood Pressure

Continued high blood pressure can put a person at risk for a stroke or heart attack. It may indicate arteriosclerosis or hardening of the arteries. Every time you go to the doctor, he or she should check your blood pressure. Many pharmacies and supermarkets have devices with which you can check your own blood pressure at no cost. You also can buy relatively inexpensive instruments to check your blood pressure at home.

Because blood pressure fluctuates throughout the day and in different settings, it is important to get a number of readings and to average them to get a true picture of your situation. This is more important for those who have had high blood pressure or those whose family health history includes heart or circulatory problems.

Blood pressure is measured using two numbers. The top number is the *systolic* pressure or the maximum pressure in the arteries when the heart beats. The lower number is the *diastolic* pressure or the pressure in the arteries between heartbeats. Following are the general guidelines for blood pressure measurements. (Check with your doctor to see what "normal" is for you, based on your family history.)

	Normal	**Borderline**	**High Blood Pressure**
Systolic	139 or less	140–159	160 or higher
Diastolic	89 or less	90–104	105 or higher

It is a good idea to check your blood pressure periodically and bring the record of your measurements with you to your annual physical.

Just for Him

Okay, men, now that the ladies are no longer reading this, let's talk. There are a couple of issues unique to us that need to be discussed. Don't be embarrassed—it's just us.

Impotence

Impotence, technically called *erectile dysfunction,* is defined as the inability to achieve and sustain an erection. The good news is impotence is nearly 100 percent correctable.

Most men will face this issue at some point. The National Institutes of Health (NIH) estimate that it affects 10–20 million men in the United States. Approximately 25 percent of men over 65 have this problem. For years, men have thought of erectile dysfunction as an embarrassment. We would rather run from it than confront it and solve it. But if former Senator Robert Dole can do national commercials discussing impotence, certainly you can talk to your doctor about it.

The causes of erectile dysfunction can be either psychological or physical. The majority (80 percent) are physical. The most common physical causes are the use of drugs and medications; blood flow problems; nerve impulse problems; post-surgical problems from prostate, bladder, or rectal surgery; serious health problems; and low hormone levels. The psychological problems causing impotence are usually depression, stress, or performance anxiety.

Despite the cause, erectile dysfunction is relatively easy to diagnose and fix. See an urologist to discuss treatment or, if you're more comfortable, talk to your doctor first and ask him or her to refer you to an urologist. Costs for diagnosis and treatment are covered under Medicare, so why put it off?

Counseling usually will resolve any psychological problems causing impotence. Remedies for the physical causes of erectile dysfunction include vacuum pumps, injections, penile implants, and medication. New medications, such as Viagra, are coming on the market each year. There are risks, however, with these medications, especially for heart patients. As with any medication, talk to your doctor about your health history before you take something like Viagra.

Shortly after Viagra hit the market, I was having my annual physical. I asked the nurse if they were getting a lot of calls for the drug. She said yes and added that most of the calls were coming from wives. Why would the women call and not the men? I believe it's partly because our male egos do not want to admit we have a problem, because we are embarrassed, and because our "maleness" is questioned. Women also call because they want physical intimacy as long as they live—we all do! It is immensely pleasurable as well as healthy. Don't let your pride keep you from having a full and wonderful relationship with your beloved. You can be sexually active and fulfilled until the day you die, if you take care of yourself and deal with problems as they occur.

One problem associated with impotence is a loss of intimacy. An impotent man may avoid sexual contact for fear his wife will consider him "over the hill" or less a man than he was. At the same time, his wife may consider his impotence and lack of desire a sign that she is no longer attractive to him. Each avoids the other for the wrong reasons and a close marital relationship can soon spiral out of control. Don't let this happen to you. By the way, men, impotence may be a once or twice thing and not a long-term problem. You only need to see a doctor if the problem persists. Also remember that you can have a loving, fulfilling lovemaking experience where both partners have orgasms without a full erection or penetration.

Sex in our senior years will change somewhat, but some of the changes can be big pluses. For men, erections will take a little longer to achieve, the time to reach orgasm and ejaculate will take more time, and after an orgasm, it will take longer before we can have another one. (If you want to see the problems women have, peek at the section Jackie wrote for them.) The slower time to full erection and orgasm can be a blessing in disguise because it can provide us more time in foreplay. Women often ask us to cuddle, hug, and make them feel loved and cherished. One of the problems we men have in our youth is that we want to get to orgasm too fast, then conclude the lovemaking just when the women are getting warmed up. Retirement allows us to spend more loving time together.

Another advantage of lovemaking in retirement is that we

can do it when we feel like it and when we have the most energy. The latter is usually mid-morning. When we have families, kids, and work, the only time we have to ourselves is at night when the kids are in bed. This is also the time when we are the most tired, and bed and sleep often are more attractive than lovemaking. In retirement, we can make love anytime. Use the change to enhance your love life.

Our pastor's father, who is 80, just remarried after his first wife died from a lingering illness. He married a woman he has known for many years who is also in her 80s. She has never been married. For a wedding present, his children reserved the honeymoon suite at a nice hotel. Now that's a success story! We can have love and a full life even when we are *old-old!*

Prostate Cancer

This is another health concern we men don't like to talk about. Now that several celebrities have "gone public" about their bouts with prostate cancer, it may be a little easier for men to discuss this serious illness.

The prostate gland is located between the penis and the rectum. It produces semen, which is mixed with the sperm from the testes and is ejaculated when we have an orgasm. As we age, the prostate has a tendency to enlarge, and, in some men, it can become cancerous. Not all enlarged prostates are cancerous; they need not be treated unless they are causing problems.

Signs of an enlarged prostate include slow and difficult urination, a frequent need to get up at night to urinate, and an urgency to urinate that produces little urine. These symptoms are caused by the enlarged prostate pushing on the bladder and urethra. If you experience any of these symptoms, see an urologist. There are new drugs that show promise of reducing prostate growth. There also is a relatively minor surgical procedure called a transurethral prostatectomy (TURP) that can relieve these problems. In this procedure, the doctor goes in through the penis, without making an incision, and removes some sections of the prostate, reducing it in size but leaving it intact.

Your doctor should check your prostate during your annual physical using two different tests. In the first, he places a finger in your rectum to feel whether the prostate is enlarged. The second is a blood test. The doctor will order a PSA test that can give evidence as to whether the prostate is cancerous. If the PSA is positive, your doctor may wish to do a biopsy to confirm the findings.

If the prostate is cancerous, your doctor may recommend some of the new treatments that are less invasive than removing the organ. Removal of the prostate is a last resort. However, if surgery is necessary, newer techniques maintain penile nerve connections, preserving the erection and orgasmic functions that earlier surgeries had destroyed. As with most cancers, the key is early detection because prostate cancer, if left untreated, can spread to other parts of the body, which could be fatal.

There. That wasn't so bad, was it? Let me reiterate one thing: If you are experiencing any of the symptoms we just talked about, don't hesitate to talk to your doctor, even if it's a little embarrassing.

Just for Her

Now that the men have left, ladies, we can talk about some problems that face us.

Heart Disease

Until recently, we generally thought of heart disease as a man's problem. Many women are still shocked to find out that it is the main cause of death in women. Even as this illness takes its toll, marvelous new methods of detection and treatment are now available. Electron Beam Computerized Tomography (EBCT), an ultra-fast CAT scan, takes quick, clear pictures of the body. Its stop-action photos "freeze" the heart in motion, allowing doctors to locate calcium deposits in the coronary arteries, a common precursor to the plaque that eventually can lead to a heart attack. This scan detects early signs of heart disease with 95 percent accuracy—a much higher rate than that of standard, non-invasive tests. Although critics point out that not every case of severe arteriosclerosis involves significant calcium deposits, they agree that the EBCT is a major advance.

A step toward early detection is to know your family history. Keep a log of family members who have had heart disease and related ailments and share it with your doctor. He or she also can give you free brochures on heart disease. Or you can get free information from the American Heart Association and the National Health Information Center (1-800-336-4797). Be familiar with the symptoms of heart disease—preventive maintenance is the key to a healthy heart.

Breast and Cervical Cancers

Breast and cervical cancers are particular problems for women, especially if cancer runs in the family. We have to be diligent about doing a monthly breast self-examination. These five precious minutes each month may ultimately give you many additional years of a healthy, happy life. Find a "buddy" and remind each other to do this exam on a certain day each month. If you are unsure of the proper procedure, your doctor's office can give you a pamphlet and a laminated card to hang in your shower. The card shows you how to examine yourself and reminds you when to do it. If you are postmenopausal, check with your doctor for the best day of the month to perform your exam.

In addition to this simple step, be sure to get an annual checkup that includes a blood test, Pap smear, bone density test, and a mammogram. These tests are relatively painless, covered by most medical insurance, and are vital to your mental and physical health. If you haven't had a physical in more than a year, STOP. Get on the phone and make that important call. Beating breast and cervical cancer depends on early detection.

Osteoporosis

Menopause produces a variety of changes in women. Those nagging "hot flashes" are perhaps the first sign. Bring on the estrogen replacement, please! Research shows the use of such replacement hormones (Premarin, Provera, and Prempro, to name a few) aids in the deceleration of bone thinning.

Bone strength gradually declines after the third decade of life. Caucasian women, smokers, women of slight build, sedentary women, and those whose diets are deficient in calcium have higher incidence of osteoporosis. Women are placed at greater risk for bone fractures if estrogen replacement is not used. Common fractures are in the hip, spine, wrist, and ankle. Hip fractures especially are a serious medical problem for older women.

Screenings for osteoporosis are available. Ask your doctor for a bone density test at your next physical exam. The risk of osteoporosis can be reduced significantly if you exercise regularly, stop smoking, and take hormone replacement therapy.

Vaginal Dryness

Vaginal dryness is a minor problem in menopausal women. It can be treated easily with vaginal creams, readily available in most drug stores. These creams can assist in reducing discomfort during intercourse. If the creams don't seem to help, discuss the problem with your doctor.

Loving Sexual Relationships

The need for human affection is ageless. An active sexual relationship with your mate does not have to cease because of age. The children are grown, your estrogen replacement is working, and time is available to enjoy each other with few distractions. God has given us this wonderful feeling called love. It can be expressed in so many ways: making love leisurely in the daytime, sitting in the spa, going to a movie, dining out, traveling, renewing friendships that have lapsed. Jim and I have set aside Friday night as "Italian night." Create your own special time with your husband—going to a ball game, listening to music, whatever the two of you enjoy.

With the love of God first in your heart, your golden days will be better than ever!

For Men and Women

Okay. Now that we've had our private talks, let us say this: If you would like further information on any of the topics we just discussed, it is easily available on the Internet. If you do not have a computer, go to a friend's home or ask your children (even grandchildren) for help. Look up some of the websites listed under "health" in our list of *Websites for Seniors* in Appendix D on page 149.

We sincerely hope you are fully committed to doing everything possible to live a healthy life. It is well worth it. As Scripture teaches, our bodies are "temple[s] of the Holy Spirit" (1 Corinthians 6:19). In the next verse, we are told to "honor God with your body" (1 Corinthians 6:20). We honor God when we keep His "temple" in good shape. Consider the promises from our gracious and loving heavenly Father on the following page as you reflect on your health in your retirement years.

He said, "If you listen carefully to the voice of the LORD your God and do what is right in His eyes, if you pay attention to His commands and keep all His decrees, I will not bring on you any of the diseases I brought on the Egyptians, for I am the LORD who heals you." (Exodus 15:26)

Worship the LORD your God, and His blessing will be on your food and water. I will take away sickness from among you. (Exodus 23:25)

Dear friend, I pray that you may enjoy good health and that all may go well with you, even as your soul is getting along well. (3 John 1:2)

three

ACTIVITY

Finding New Meaning in Life

Some think they are busy
when they are only confused.

[Jesus said,] "For My yoke is easy and My burden is light."
(Matthew 11:30)

Saturday was always an active day in our family. We did things and went places. There was no time for resting—we did that on Sunday. Retirement should be active as well. The difference between pre- and post-retirement should not be less activity, but the freedom to do those things you most want to do.

Be warned: Retirement can be dangerous to your health if you are not active and if you do not find meaningful things to do. As we mentioned earlier, many people find all meaning in life in their jobs, and, once they retire, they lose their reason to live. On the other hand, here are some prime examples of people who have "done it right." Former President Jimmy Carter is doing wonderful things in retirement. Are you handy with tools? Do you like building things? Do you like the feeling you get from helping those less fortunate than you? Then you may want to join Mr. Carter in the Habitat for Humanity program.

Maybe you're not looking for something so strenuous. Dwight Eisenhower and Winston Churchill both took up painting when they retired. Both were involved in activities—such as writing—that made life better for those who followed them. Colonel Sanders started Kentucky Fried Chicken *after* he retired. There are countless stories of people who saw retirement not as a time to stop and sit, but as a time to refocus on meaningful activity. So the question is not *should* you find something to do, but *what* does God want you to do?

God's yoke is easy, as Scripture says. He invites us to use the talents He has given us, however few or many they may be. When we are doing the things God has gifted us to do, they are easy and even fun. It is not unusual to hear successful people say they love to go to work. That's because when they are doing what they are gifted to do, it is fun and fulfilling. If you already have a good handle on your gifts, the key is putting them to use, perhaps in a volunteer program. If you don't know what your gifts are, talk to your pastor. He might be able to help you with a "gifts assessment" program and point you toward some appropriate activities.

Warning: Becoming over-committed in activities you do not like and are not gifted to do is a sure way to cast a pall over your retirement. Do not be afraid to say no to people who want you to do things you are not gifted to do. Also avoid giving long commitments to any program unless you are certain it is something you will love and enjoy. Save time for yourself and for doing those things that will recharge your batteries. Find a good balance between recreation and meaningful activity. Need some ideas? Here some things other seniors have found meaningful.

Computers

We are in the Information Age. No device is more important today than the computer. And none can so enrich your retirement. You literally can sit in your home and have the world of information at your fingertips.

You can send electronic mail (e-mail) to anyone, anywhere in the world, at no cost (provided he or she also has Internet access). You can read newspapers from all over the world, do research, meet new people, study the Bible, read Christian magazines, get daily Christian quotations, trace your family history, play games, get investment information, and do a host of other things—most at no cost—once you are connected to the Internet. And that's just the beginning. New technology is being developed almost constantly, and the beauty of the computer world is that things get cheaper and more "user friendly" every day.

People don't fail, they give up trying.

If you are not familiar with computers, and do not have a close friend or relative to teach you how to use one, there are many places you can learn. Most community colleges offer free or reduced-tuition courses to seniors so you can learn how to use the computer and various software applications. The American Association of Retired Persons (AARP) sponsors free workshops across the country in conjunction with Microsoft Corporation to help seniors get up to speed in the Information Age. Many companies, vocational schools, and adult education programs also offer programs. There is a massive educational effort underway to train Americans to use computers. Take advantage of it!

If taking a class or workshop isn't feasible, bookstores are filled with books that will provide you with the

"He used to love running on the beach, chasing squirrels, catching a ball. That was before I got a computer."

information you need to get started. Many people have never had formal training yet use the computer effectively. Jackie and I taught ourselves; it's not hard. Just find a book that presents the basics in a clear manner, preferably with many pictures of computer screens so you can follow along easily.

Some Basics about Computers

Drives

A computer normally has three types of drives installed:

- **CD-ROM Drive**—This drive uses a removable compact disc (CD), which has data that the computer reads and processes. A CD is capable of storing a large amount of data. For example, an entire encyclopedia can be stored on one CD. The *ROM* in CD-ROM stands for Read Only Memory, which means you cannot *write* data to the CD; you can only *read* data. Most computer programs you purchase today are on CDs.

- **Floppy Drive**—This drive uses a removable diskette called a *floppy disk*. (So named because in the early days of computers, the diskette was made of a flexible or "floppy" material.) The *floppy drive* differs from the *CD-ROM drive* in that you can read and write to and from disks using this drive. The *floppy disk*, however, cannot store as much data as a CD. You also can copy data from your computer onto a *floppy disk* and store it or pass it on to someone else.

- **Hard Drive**—The *hard drive* is the main data storage device in your computer. The computer's *Operating System* software—as well as all program software—is loaded onto this drive. When you create a letter or other document and want to save it, it is stored by default on your *hard drive*. (If you want to save it to a *floppy disk*, you can do that as well.) When you load software applications from your *CD-ROM drive* or your *floppy drive,* the software is stored on your *hard drive.* You can write to or read data from your *hard drive.*

Software

Software is digital data, generally recorded on a diskette or CD, which tells the computer how to operate and to perform certain tasks. Basically, *software* is a set of instructions for the computer. Think about music being recorded on a phonograph record, cassette tape, or CD. The computer records its data in much the same way, but the data is *digital* (ones and zeros).

There are two types of *software* used in computers: *operating system* (OS) and *application software* (also referred to as *programs*). Think of *software* as something you can't touch or see, just as you cannot touch or see the music on your record, tape, or CD.

- **Operating System (OS)**—This is the general set of digital instructions necessary for the computer to operate. It determines how the computer will present its data. The first major OS, named DOS (Disk Operating System), was developed by Bill Gates, the founder of Microsoft. DOS and *Windows* are used by more than 80 percent of the world's *personal computers* (PCs). You may have heard of *Windows, Windows 95, Windows 98,* or *Windows NT.* These software products also were developed by Microsoft and are *Graphical User Interfaces* (GUI, pronounced "gooey"). *Windows* functions "on top of" DOS. Think of DOS as the engine of your car. You don't look at your car's engine when you start your car, but it is there, functioning, nonetheless. Instead, you put your key in the ignition and turn it. *Windows* is the more user-friendly key and ignition. It's a series of "menus" and "buttons" at which you point and click your *mouse* to make the computer's "engine" run. As of this writing, the latest version is *Windows 2000*; however, new versions can be expected every two years or so.

- **Application Software (Programs)**—This software is written to perform a specific task. It works in conjunction with the *OS* to accomplish its task. For example, if you want to play the card game Solitaire on your computer, you will need to purchase a *software program* that includes Solitaire. (Actually, Solitaire comes pre-loaded on most computers—this is just for illustration purposes.) This *software* will tell the computer how to play the game and present the game to you on the *monitor* so you can play. Similarly, if you want to write a letter, get on the Internet, or install an encyclopedia on your computer, you need to purchase *application software* (word processing software, Internet service provider software, or an encyclopedia on CD-ROM, respectively) that will enable you to do these tasks.

Hardware

Where *software* are the parts of the computer you *can't* see or touch, *hardware* are the parts you *can* see and touch. There are four pieces of *hardware* you *must* have for your computer to function: *a central processing unit (CPU), a monitor, a keyboard, and a mouse.* There are also many other optional pieces of *hardware,* such as *external hard drives, microphones, external speakers, printers,* etc. Let's look at the necessary pieces. If you're interested in adding some of the optional pieces, get information on them from an introductory book on computers or ask about them at a computer store.

- **Central Processing Unit (CPU)**—The *CPU* (sometimes called simply a *processor*) reads instructions from the *OS* and from the *programs,* then manipulates and processes the data received to yield the desired output. Think of the *CPU* as the brain of the computer, only without memory. If something must be "remembered," it is stored on the *hard drive*. The speed of the *processor* determines how quickly the computer can accomplish its tasks. This speed is referred to in *Megahertz* (MHZ), such as 166 MHZ, 200 MHZ, 400 MHZ, etc. The higher the number of MHZ, the faster the computer will process data.

- **Monitor**—The *monitor* is the part that looks like your TV. It allows you to see what is happening on your computer. The *monitor* doesn't do anything by itself; it's merely a conduit for you to see the result of what the computer is processing.

- **Keyboard**—The *keyboard* looks like a flattened version of a typewriter and is used to type information into your computer. You'll notice that a computer's *keyboard* has more keys than a typewriter. The main set of keys is in the same layout as a type-writer, so if you learned to type in school, you can apply those same skills with the computer *keyboard*. The "extra" keys include *function* keys, which help you complete common com-puter functions more easily, and a *number pad*, which is set up like the number pad on an adding machine. The *number pad* is especially helpful when you use *programs* that do high-end math functions or that calculate your taxes.

- **Mouse**—The *mouse* is a device that moves the cursor (the little flashing line that appears on the *monitor*) and selects various items that appear on the *monitor*. The *mouse* helps you direct and manipulate data and choose commands from pull-down menus. Why is it called a *mouse*? It is usually gray or off-white and has a long, thin cord that connects it to the *CPU*. The cord looks like a tail; hence, the devise looks like a mouse.

The Internet

The *Internet* is a worldwide communication network using the telephone lines in your home or business to connect your computer to other computers, other networks, and other information databases. (*Note:* While current technology still uses telephone lines, new technology is already in place to use the cable from cable television as well as wireless technology used for cell phones. Regardless of how you connect to it, the *Internet's* definition doesn't change.) Just as you dial your telephone to reach someone, your computer uses the same lines to dial in and connect with the *Internet*—and a host of information on literally every subject. The *Internet* is a huge network of computers all over the world, sharing information. When it was created, it was used by the military to share classified information. But Tim Berners Lee created a computer language called HTML because he envisioned that it could make the *Internet* a free resource for anyone who wanted to share information globally.

Important Terms

Following are some terms you should know as you begin to work with a computer.

- **HTML (Hypertext Mark-up Language)**—A computer language that creates electronically annotated and linked documents using *hyperlinks*. In documents, *hyperlinks* usually appear as blue, underlined text. Click on them with your mouse and you will "jump" to the linked page.

- **Laptop**—A portable computer with the ability to be battery operated.

- **Modem**—A device used to connect a computer to a phone line. Most PCs have *internal modems* into which you can plug a phone line.

- **Peripherals**—Hardware components that connect to computers to perform special functions. Examples are *printers, scanners, cameras,* and *speakers.*

- **PC**—Stands for *personal computer.*

- **Ports**—Connecting points located on a *processor circuit board* into which *peripherals,* such as *modems, printers,* and *scanners,* can be plugged.

- **Printer**—A *peripheral* device that permits the operator to print data from the computer on paper. Printers come in various types, such as *dot matrix* (rarely used anymore), *ink jet, bubble jet,* and *laser.*

- **RAM (Random Access Memory)**—A type of memory the computer uses to process information. It is short-term memory. The information stored in *RAM* is available only as long as the computer is on. Turn the computer off, and the information in *RAM* is deleted.

- **Slots and Bays**—Receptacles in a *processor circuit board* into which new devices (*video* and *sound cards*) can be placed to upgrade a computer system.

- **Scanner**—A *peripheral* device that permits the transfer of printed material into the computer where it can be added to documents, manipulated, or stored as a file. A *scanner* literally takes a picture of the document you are scanning and makes it a *digital image.* For example, you can scan a picture of your grandchildren, add a caption to it, and e-mail it to your friends, making yourself an electronic "brag book."

- **Sound Card**—An internal *card* that allows the computer to convert data into sound. If you have a *sound card* in your computer and speakers, you can play music, hear sounds recorded on websites, and play games with sound effects.

- **Video Card**—An internal *card* that turns data into images on the computer screen. Some videos and games may require a more sophisticated *video card* than is standard.

- **VRAM**—Type of *memory* a computer's *video card* uses to "draw" pictures more quickly.

- **World Wide Web**—The part of the *Internet* that displays *HTML pages*. These pages permit the use of *hypertext*, which allows you to move from one *web page* to another with a simple mouse click.

I'm Retired. Why Should I Own a Computer?

It doesn't matter how old you are, if you do not have a computer, get one. Many retirees report that they have improved significantly the quality of their retirement years by learning to use a computer. Worried about the price? As technology advances, prices drop. As of this writing, you can get a good PC for well under $1,000 and an adequate one for under $500, often with a good printer as part of the deal. You also can get good deals on used computers from people who are upgrading. Check newspaper want ads, bulletin boards in supermarkets, and computer stores that specialize in rebuilding older computers.

Find someone you trust who knows something about computers to help you shop. Don't let some salesperson talk you into the top of the line if you're only going to use the computer to send e-mail to your grandkids and check your investments on the Internet. Think about what you'll be using the computer for before you purchase one. Your usage plans will determine the type and "size" of machine you'll need. For example, you'll need a faster, "bigger" computer if you plan to design your own website, publish a newsletter for your gardening club, maintain a database for your church, keep track of your finances in a program such as Quicken, etc. You'll need to do a little research on the current "speeds" and "sizes" of computers. For example, as of this writing, we would recommend the following as *minimum* requirements for a new computer.

— 400 MHZ; more is better.

— 32 megabytes (MB) of RAM; go for 64 if you can afford it.

— A 2 gigabyte (GIG) hard drive or better.

— At least 2 MB of VRAM.

— 12x or better CD-ROM drive. Faster is better; go to 24x if you can.

— A 56 Kbps internal modem that meets the v.90 standard. Speed is very important here, but it is limited by how fast data can be transmitted over your phone lines and the speed of your Internet provider's interface.

— A 15-inch monitor is standard. If you have vision problems, get a 17-inch monitor.

— A 3 or 4 bay computer case leaves plenty of room for upgrades and expansion.

— A Windows 98 operating system or the latest available.

— An inkjet or bubble jet color printer.

Because technology changes so rapidly, use the specifications above as a guide for a minimum setup. By the time you read this, you may well be able to get much more for your money. Generally speaking, more is better in computers, so if you can get more speed, memory, screen size, etc., get it. You won't be sorry.

So far we've been talking about PCs, which generally refers to computers made by IBM and "IBM compatible" computers made by other companies. The other "kind" of personal computer is made by Apple Computers (often called a MAC, short for Macintosh). Apple computers are somewhat more user-friendly, but 90 percent of the machines in use are IBM compatibles. This means that most software programs are written for IBM compatibles, not MACs. Some of the reputable companies making IBM compatibles are Gateway, Compaq, Dell, AST, Micron, Packard Bell, and, of course, IBM. Look for the best deal.

Once you have your computer, you'll want to get on the Internet. To do so, you will need a phone line to plug into your machine. Some people have a separate, dedicated line installed just to connect to the Internet. Others get a split plug and use the main phone line. If you use your main line, however, you will not be able to place or receive calls while you are online. Either way, you need Touch-Tone service, and if you have call waiting or some other phone features, they may interrupt modem transmission. Ask your salesperson if you are in doubt.

Next, you need to get an *Internet Service Provider* (ISP) with a local or 800 phone number so when your computer dials into the ISP's computer, you do not have additional phone charges. Most ISPs will charge from $12.00 to $19.95 a month for unlimited service, depending on whether you sign up for one, two, or three years. Once you install your ISP's software, your computer will be able to dial up their computer and take you to their website.

With a phone connection and an ISP, you are free to enter the marvelous world of information on the "Information Superhighway." The Internet contains millions of web pages (current estimates say 100,000 new pages come online each week). An address for a web page will look like this: **http://www.cph.org**. Most addresses are preceded with **http://**,

which stands for *hypertext transfer protocol*. With most *browsers*—
such as Internet Explorer or Netscape—you no longer need to
type **http://** because it's done for you. So we'll concern ourselves
with the part of the addresses after the http://. The *www* stands
for World Wide Web. The letters following the *www* are the
name, or abbreviation of the name, of the web page owner or
the server on which the page resides. The *cph* happens to be an
abbreviation of the name of our publisher, Concordia
Publishing House. And the *org* is the domain where the web
page is located. *Org* is an abbreviation for *nonprofit organization*.
Other popular domains are for commercial ventures (*com*), educational institutions (*edu*), and the government (*gov*). Each
nation on the Internet also has a domain designation, such as
the United States (*us*), Canada (*ca*), France (*fr*), and Germany
(*de*).

Website addresses must be typed in correctly or they won't
work. Pay attention to letter case and the punctuation. (Unlike
addressing an envelope where, if you misspell a street name, the
post office will likely be able to deliver it, on the Internet, if you
make a typographical error, the computer won't be able to find
the "address.") In Appendix D, you will find a list of websites of
particular interest to seniors.

Electronic mail (*e-mail*) is one of the marvels of the Internet.
You can send messages at no cost to anyone, anywhere in the
world. E-mail is fast replacing regular, first-class mail (called
"snail mail" by the computer savvy) for sending messages. It can
be sent instantaneously, and, if you so desire, you can send the
same message to a group of people with one click of the mouse
(provided you have listed their addresses in your electronic
address book, a file system to store and coordinate individual
and group e-mail addresses).

E-mail addresses look something like website addresses. Once you become proficient at "reading" e-mail addresses, they'll tell you all about the person you are e-mailing. An e-mail address has the person's (or organization's) "name," followed by the symbol @ (which stands for "at"), then the ISP's address (where the person receives his or her e-mail) and the server's domain location. For example, our e-mail address is jharvey@olg.com. To break that down, it's a form of our name (a first initial and the full last name), then @, then our ISP's name, which is an abbreviation of On-line Gateway, then their domain. On-line Gateway happens to be commercial, so its domain is *com*. Some addresses get a little more complicated. For example, if a teacher at a public school could receive e-mail at school, her e-mail address might look something like this: jrsmith@vvsd.k12.mo.us. Can you decipher it? That's J.R. Smith (teacher's name) at Valley View School District (organization's name) *dot* K–12 (the designation for a school with grades kindergarten through 12) *dot* Missouri (the state) *dot* United States (the country). Seem confusing? With a little practice, you'll get used to it.

But What Will I Use the Internet for besides E-mail?

The computer truly opens up a new world right in your home. You can get software that allows you to search the Bible in remarkable ways. You can type in a key word and have the computer list every passage in the Bible using that word. With another click of the mouse, you can see the passages themselves. You can play chess, bridge, and hundreds of other games by yourself, with someone at home, or with someone across the world. You can find information on almost any subject, which brings us to the topic of *search engines*.

Because the Internet is huge and the amount of data vast,

there is software to help you find what you want. These devices are called *search engines.* On your ISP's home page, you likely will find the word *search* or *searches.* Clicking on that word will give you a choice of several *search engines.* (A list of the most popular ones is in Appendix D.) At a *search engine* website, you will find a place to type in a word or phrase relating to the topic you are interested in researching. You also will find a *button* to click on named "search." Once you type what you're looking for and click "search," the software will scan the Internet and show you a list of websites containing the words for which you searched. It will even attempt to rank them in the order that they'll be useful to you. Each *search engine* also will give you instructions for limiting searches so you get exactly the information or sites for which you are looking.

Search engines can be powerful tools. Recently, Jim was working on an article that dealt with the *Roe v. Wade* Supreme Court decision on abortion. He wanted to find Ms. Roe's first name, so he went to an Internet search engine. He typed in "Roe v. Wade" and got a list of possible related websites. He clicked on one that seemed promising, and, with another click, he was actually listening to the case being argued before the Supreme Court. He couldn't believe his ears. He was hearing the actual arguments being made when the case was before the court. History was brought alive in our home that day—and he learned a valuable lesson about the power of the Internet.

"I want my husband to pay more attention to me. Got any perfume that smells like a computer?"

No instrument can open up the world of information better than the computer. It will allow you to study, communicate, be entertained, and even work at home, if you wish. You're already living in the Information Age—take advantage of it.

Working

The opportunities for seniors to work have never been greater. Whether you need extra money, simply enjoy working, or want to maintain associations with colleagues, work is a viable option. The good news is that most employers want older workers because studies show they are more reliable.

Some seniors continue working part-time for their former employers as consultants, perhaps even sharing a job with another senior. Others continue working full-time, but in a different capacity after they "retire." If you are interested in continuing to work and want to look at opportunities, there are many helpful websites. For example, Lycos Careers at **www.lycos.com/careers** offers help in looking for jobs and preparing resumes. It also provides links to other websites.

Some seniors start their own companies and work full- or part-time. Many seniors, who are professionals in certain fields, teach part-time or start their own consulting businesses. Others make their hobbies into money-making enterprises. Art, photography, handicrafts, and collectibles are all hobbies that can become money-makers.

Still other seniors purchase a franchise. While a purchase of this magnitude requires careful research, a franchise can provide a marvelous way to work at something you enjoy and add to your income. Information on franchises can be found in several places. The Federal Trade Commission regulates franchises, so there is data and information at its website: **www.ftc.gov**. The American Franchisee Association (AFA) also has a website with information and links to numerous other websites: **www.vaxxine.com/franchise/afa/afa2.html**. If you prefer to write this organization, the address is AFA, 53 W. Jackson, Suite 205, Chicago, Illinois 60604. The phone number is (321) 431-0545.

Volunteering

One of the wonderful ways to spend time, make a contribution, stay active, and make new friends is to volunteer for a charity. There are thousands of charities that would love to have your help.

He is no fool who gives what he cannot keep to gain what he cannot lose.

Nearly every community has a literacy council that sponsors programs to help people learn to read. These programs are almost always looking for volunteers. Most communities also have a "meals-on-wheels" program that delivers meals to shut-ins. These programs often need people to serve as drivers. There are also hospice programs that need volunteers to assist the dying and their families.

For retired executives, the National Executive Service Corps (NESC) offers free consulting services to nonprofit organizations. You can reach the organization's headquarters at 257 Park Ave. South, NY, NY 10010–7304. Another opportunity for retired executives is the Service Corps of Retired Executives (SCORE). It provides consulting services to small businesses. Currently 12,400 people across the country are involved with SCORE in helping start and manage small businesses. This group can be found on the Internet at **www.score.org**. The phone number is 1-800-634-0245. SCORE cooperates with the Small Business Administration (SBA) of the federal government. Its website address is **www.sba.gov**.

Habitat for Humanity, a volunteer program started by former President Jimmy Carter, builds homes for the poor and needy. Habitat for Humanity trains its volunteers and provides the materials. It is a wonderful way to travel and live your faith at the same time. If you are interested in more information, you can contact the program at Habitat for Humanity, 121 Habitat St., Americus, GA 31709. The phone number is (912) 924-6935, and its website is **www.habitat.org**.

Elderhostel is another program that offers numerous travel-linked volunteer opportunities related to community development, archaeology, environmental research, historic preservation, conservation, and teaching/tutoring. (See the travel section that follows for information on how to contact them for a free catalog.)

Local prisons and correctional facilities are also looking for volunteers. The chaplains often need Bible study leaders, and there are usually opportunities to teach and tutor inmates. You may wish to work with Charles Colson's Prison Fellowship Ministry, Angel Tree Ministry, or Neighbors Who Care Ministry, all of which can be found at his website: **www.pfm.org**.

When it comes to giving,
some people will stop at nothing.

Obviously, your local church is a good place to start volunteer activity. Use your creativity to suggest new ministries to your church leaders. Jim suggested a new ministry in sign evangelism at our church. This ministry places messages of truth on our church sign. These messages reach hundreds of people who drive by our church every day. This led to a marvelous outreach in our community and to Jim's new book, *701 Sentence Sermons,* published by Kregel Publications. (Another good book on the subject, published by Concordia, is *Signs for These Times* by Ronald Glusenkamp.)

Pray that God will provide new opportunities for you to serve Him using your gifts, then step back and watch Him open up doors for you. For example, we heard about a woman whose husband had died and she was looking for volunteer opportunities. She decided to combine her love for children and her love for travel as a volunteer nanny for missionaries. She now travels the world, fulfilling a real need, meeting new people, caring for children, and visiting exciting new places. At a church we visited recently, several men who love to work on cars started a ministry to repair old cars for single mothers and those in need. They advertise for donated cars (for which the donors receive a tax break), then fix them up and give them to those in need. The men get together at the church during the week, have fellowship together, enjoy working on cars, and help those in need. That's a win-win proposition.

We can't begin to scratch the surface of the opportunities for volunteer service. Opportunities are available in schools, hospitals, prisons, and many other places. You will find more volunteer opportunities at some of the websites listed in Appendix D.

More than one senior has told us it seems like their life experiences prior to retiring prepared them for serving God more effectively in retirement. We feel that way too. Do you see the significance of that attitude? It means God has been preparing us to do special work for Him in retirement. It means perhaps the most important work we will do in this life is what we will do for Him in retirement. So retirement is not the end of a life but the beginning of something marvelous that will only get better. And you will be healthier, happier, and will make a significant difference in the lives of others.

My boss is a Jewish carpenter.

Public Service

An important area where seniors can "give back" and make a difference is the exercising of citizenship rights and responsibilities. The extra time we have available can be used to study public issues and get involved in helping to set public policy. We have more time to read the newspapers, watch C-Span, and study issues so we can become more informed voters or even elected officials. We also bring broad experience and an historical perspective that is important to our democratic process.

You may wish to run for elected office and serve as a public official. Or you may wish to volunteer to assist candidates running for office. No candidate or political party will turn down someone willing to do volunteer work. You also can be a poll watcher or work for the board of elections part-time during election season when additional people are needed. There are numerous ways to get involved.

As Christians, when we become involved in public affairs, we have the broad perspective of working for the benefit of all people rather than pushing a selfish seniors' agenda. True, we need to pay attention to issues such as social security and Medicare, but we also should have a balanced view. As a senior, you have potent political power—use it wisely.

Travel and Education

We'll discuss these two topics together because they are frequently combined activities for seniors. Many travel/study programs offered for seniors are a marvelous combination of learning, travel, and making new friends. And more seniors than ever are going back to school—particularly college—to gain new knowledge, skills, and even degrees. Close to 100,000 seniors are enrolled in college courses each year. Community colleges have made a special effort to reach out to seniors with low-cost or free courses and specially designed programs, including ones that allow you first to study about an area, then travel to it.

The primary travel/study organization for seniors is Elderhostel, a marvelous group that catalogs thousands of travel/study opportunities for seniors. These low-cost programs allow seniors of all income levels to travel all over the United States and the world with other seniors, learning, socializing, and having a great time. You can get Elderhostel's free catalogs by

TRAVEL AGENCY

GLASBERGEN

"Someplace hot enough to melt my fat away the moment I step on to the beach."

© 1998 RANDY GLASBERGEN.

writing to them at Elderhostel, 75 Federal St., Boston, MA 02110. The group's website is **www.elderhostel.org**.

Many Elderhostel programs around the world are based at colleges and universities and use the same faculties and facilities. Other programs are based at camps and conference centers. Still others accommodate participants in hotels and motels. As mentioned earlier, many of the programs involve volunteer work, particularly preserving wildlife and the environment. We urge you to try this marvelous way to learn, travel, meet new friends, and have fun.

One of our favorite ways to travel is on a cruise. You can see wonderful places during the day and be entertained or educated at night, all without the packing and unpacking of other modes of travel. On a cruise, you take your hotel, dining room, and entertainment with you as you travel the world. Cruises often have themes as well. Some emphasize sports, music, business, or investment issues. There are also Christian cruises where Bible study and Christian music are featured.

If you are looking for travel bargains, you will find several websites listed under *travel* in Appendix D. Some cruise lines cater to an older crowd, so be sure to ask your friends and travel agents which ones might best meet your needs.

Other seniors rent or purchase recreational vehicles (RVs) and travel the country meeting new people, visiting old friends, and having a wonderful time. Still others rent houseboats and travel inland waterways. It's a great way to travel, fish, meet new people, and see places you wouldn't otherwise see.

Senior Organizations

There are two primary organizations serving seniors. The newest one and one we recommend for all Christian seniors is the Christian Association of PrimeTimers (CAPS). The other is the American Association of Retired People (AARP). Both offer numerous travel and insurance discounts to members. Both CAPS and AARP charge low annual fees for senior couples. Check with them for the current rates. You can join CAPS by writing to: Christian Association of PrimeTimers, P.O. Box 777, St. Charles, Illinois 60174. You can join AARP by writing to: American Association of Retired People, 601 E St. N.W., Washington, D.C. 20049.

AARP is very political and likely has the strongest lobbying operation in Washington, D.C. It is committed to using big government to protect the interests of seniors. This is partially why CAPS was started. We belong to both so we can be associated with fellow Christians and stay in touch with what AARP says it is doing on our behalf.

Both of these organizations provide seniors with discounts for products and services, but buyer beware—just because it's discounted doesn't mean it's the best product or service available. This is especially true with insurance. When purchasing insurance, make sure you get at least two other quotes. And note that nearly every hotel and motel in the country will give seniors at least 10 percent off, even if you don't belong to one of these organizations. Good deals for seniors, therefore, begin with discounts above 10 percent.

American businesses are kind to seniors in a variety of ways, including discounting prices for senior citizens on many products and services. Never hesitate to ask whether a restaurant, theater, store, or other commercial enterprise has a senior discount. It's the businesses' way of saying "thank you" to us for our services and a way to help us stretch our retirement dollars.

Time

Each of us has a limited amount of time in life. Time lost is gone forever. Does this mean we shouldn't enjoy ourselves, take vacations, or take time for ourselves? Of course not, but it does mean we should use our time wisely.

Consider the parable of the talents in Matthew 25:14–30. God has given each of us so many talents and so much time. While our energy decreases and our need to rest increases, God still empowers us by His Holy Spirit to do His work to the best of our ability. Talents we once used to make money now may be used for His kingdom. The additional time we have may now be used to do things we are good at and which may help others. Why spend your last 15 to 20 years of life entirely in self-serving activities? Could we justify spending all that time fishing, golfing, or watching TV when there are needs to be met, people to help, a Great Commission to be carried out? We think not. Must we spend every waking moment doing something productive? Not at all. In fact, if we did, we would soon wear out. The key is to find a good balance between service and recreation. Living our faith in service to others will help us mentally, physically, and spiritually by giving us a reason for living. The recreation will give us the energy and enjoyment to keep a sparkle in life. Finding a service area that uses your talents fully is key to making that part of retirement as joyous and fun as the recreation.

Lost time is never found again.

Using our time in retirement wisely also requires that we plan our activities around some realities. As we age, we need more time to recuperate from activity. All good recreation is just that, *re*-creation, not *wreak*-reation. Our retirement is a time to continue to live our faith as we do the tasks the Lord gives us and to mix that with leisure activities that "recharge our batteries," help us learn and grow, and enable us to serve Him even more effectively.

We believe as long as God allows us to stay here, it means He has something for us to do. If He didn't, He would bring us home. The key to a successful retirement is to find out what God wants us to do and to do it well. This will keep us active, healthy, and happy.

The righteous will flourish like a palm tree, they will grow like a cedar of Lebanon; planted in the house of the LORD, they will flourish in the courts of our God. They will still bear fruit in old age, they will stay fresh and green, proclaiming, "The LORD is upright; He is my Rock, and there is no wickedness in Him." (Psalm 92:12–15)

Effective use of time is critical to seniors. As our physical energies ebb, it becomes vitally important that we use the time and energy we have in the most efficient way. Understanding ourselves and our bodily cycles is important. For example, we all have times of the day when we are at our best mentally and physically and times when our body is recuperating and not at its peak. Knowing these cycles is important because it allows you to schedule the most important activities when you are at your top performance, allowing you to do the important things when you are at your peak.

Time wasted is existence;
used wisely it is life.

Many people have more energy at mid-morning. Some peak at mid-afternoon. Others are "night people," who perform best in the late evening or very early morning hours. For example, our bodily cycles put us at peak performance between 9 and 11 A.M. This is the time Jim uses for writing and investment work. Jackie schedules her hospice and Bible study work during this time. We use afternoons for exercise, chores, and activities with less significance. Obviously we can't always schedule things this way, but to the extent we can, we are likely to do important things better, faster, and more easily.

If you are in control of your time, you, too, can schedule your most important activities when you are at your best. If you manage time effectively, you can offset the decline in energy with more effective planning and use of time, thereby actually increasing your productive work. Working smarter rather than harder makes great sense, particularly in retirement. Think about Mother Teresa who, though slowed by heart problems in her declining years, continued to work effectively to the very end. With a little planning, every senior can make the time and energy God has given us count for more.

Sports

The longer life and better health enjoyed by modern seniors is leading to their participation in active sports even into the later years. Not only are seniors participating in sports such as golf, bowling, and tennis, but they are actively participating in baseball, basketball, and other sports once thought only for the young. There are masters tournaments in a number of sports. See Appendix D for a list. For information on other sports, go to Seniors Search on the Internet and click on *Sports and Recreation*. The website is **www.seniorssearch.com**.

Another activity for senior "jocks" that has developed recently is the "fantasy camp." Many professional sports teams now provide getaways for fans of any age where attendees can play the sport and socialize with former professional players. Jim has been to three fantasy camps offered by the Detroit Tigers. He's played baseball against some of his heroes who won World Series contests with the Tigers. Jim now has his own baseball card, tons of autographs, and many fond memories. Most of the older Major League baseball franchises have fantasy camps. Some of the National Basketball Association and National Hockey League teams do as well. To find out if your favorite professional team offers a fantasy camp, contact its public relations office.

Grandchildren

So far, we've talked about all kinds of activities in which seniors can participate, but we haven't talked much about family. We were saving one of the best activities for near the end of the chapter. The birth of a grandchild is an overwhelming experience of love. Relatives and friends get to be part of a new life.

Because you have raised your children, you are now able to transfer that experience as a parent to this new adventure.

But the role of grandparents today is different than it was for our grandparents. Years ago, grandchildren wanted to go to Grandma's house because there were so many interesting things to do and see. Grandparents were repositories of information. They had cures for almost anything that ailed you. Their answers to questions were honest and vitally important. What grandchild can't remember the wonderful smells that emanated from Grandma's kitchen? Freshly baked cookies and pies, even homemade bread, were hoped for and expected when visiting Grandma and Grandpa. Although these traits may not reflect your modern lifestyle or your interactions with your grandchildren, one thing hasn't changed. The depth of love between grandparents and grandchildren is strong and essential, a vital connection for a healthy and meaningful relationship.

Grandparents of yesteryear were basically the same from generation to generation. Their roles and responsibilities were clear-cut. Today, grandparents are faced with various obstacles. Because of the high divorce rate, single-parent households are a reality and remarriages create complex blended families. Often, both parents have to work outside the home to make ends meet. Quality childcare is hard to find, let alone afford. In many cases, grandparents are the baby-sitters today. Some even raise their grandchildren full-time.

And it isn't easy for the kids, either. They are surrounded with all types of temptations. They are pressured by their peers to experiment with drugs, engage in premarital sex at alarmingly early ages, or digress from values they've been taught, to name a few. The entire family is impacted. And the entire family isn't often around. Years ago, all generations lived near—

often *with*—one another. Today, the intergenerational family is threatened in many ways. Senior citizens move to warmer climates, putting distance between themselves and their grandchildren. They are no longer "around the corner" to help out when the younger generations need support and wisdom.

Despite the changes, it's up to us to make long-distance relationships work. Lack of proximity need not eliminate positive connections with our grandchildren. We are able to communicate with them by telephone, the Internet, or letters. Whenever possible, we can get on a plane and visit them.

We've spent this whole chapter talking about ways to stay active as seniors, but none of the activities we've mentioned is as important as being there for the family God has entrusted to your care. Let's not forget the value and importance of your input into the lives of your grandchildren. Let them know they can depend on you. Whatever your age, you have a wealth of knowledge and experience to share. Let your grandchildren know you are not perfect. Show your love and support as you pass on your wisdom. Let your age be an asset. Most of all, love your grandchildren (and their parents) with the love God the Father has shown you—a gracious love, a forgiving love, an unconditional love.

In his book, *Grandparent Power*, Arthur Kornhaber lists several roles grandparents may play in relationship to their grandchildren, including family historian, role model, teacher, mentor, student, nurturer, genie (wish grantor), crony, and hero.[6] It's important to understand these roles and to play each one when appropriate.

Grandchildren will look to you for answers in many areas. They will want to know about your parents, brothers and sisters, and other relatives. Get out the family album if you have one and tell your grandchildren stories about their heritage.

The spiritual lessons exhibited at this stage are most important. Children observe how we treat others in various situations. In all that we do, we are their role models. But we are still sinners. They need to know that we, like them, are forgiven children of our heavenly Father.

How many questions have your grandchildren asked you in the past few weeks or months? What an opportunity for us lovingly to share our insights, knowledge, and values on almost any subject. It may be hard at times, but honestly answer your grandchildren's questions. Even if it doesn't seem like a big

GLASBERGEN

"My teacher says little girls can grow up to be anything they choose! Why did you choose to be an old lady?"

© 1996 RANDY GLASBERGEN.

deal to you, it is to them or they wouldn't be asking about it. Treat them with respect, but hold your ground. Let them know you aren't perfect and don't have all the answers, but also let them see that your experience, wisdom, and faith can help keep them on the right track. Most of all, pay attention and listen. If your teenage grandson asks about smoking, tell him honestly about its hazards. Be careful, however, not to "preach"—he'll soon stop coming to you for advice. If your granddaughter confesses that she cheated on a test at school, don't dismiss her with "everyone cheats once or twice"; you're giving her license to do it again. Talk with her frankly about why cheating is a sin, but talk to her lovingly. Then offer her forgiveness.

Our grandchildren are exposed to a variety of unfavorable situations via television, movies, videos, the Internet, and more. When they visit your home, set rules about what they can watch and explain your decisions. Answer their questions honestly. Remember, your grandchildren's parents have the primary discipline responsibilities, but in your home you have the right and responsibility to enforce reasonable rules. If you and your child have serious disagreements over the discipline of your grandchildren, discuss the situation outside the presence of your grandchildren and try to reach a compromise. Your children are different parents than you were. Don't expect them to do everything the way you did it when you raised them. Be patient, loving, caring, and noncompetitive.

If God has blessed you financially and your grandchildren need assistance with college or other expenses, you may wish to help. Be careful not to do anything without the parents' prior approval (unless, of course, the parents are estranged from the children). Also use any financial assistance to build sound financial management and values in your grandchildren. For example, use loans requiring reasonable repayment over time or a gradual forgiveness of the loan based on achievement of acceptable grades or meeting agreed upon goals. Using this approach rather than an outright gift will allow you to help in their growth and development.

"Grandma, can we stay overnight at your house?" That question says you are someone special. Although grandchildren may head to the cookie jar when entering the house, it is still a warm and wonderful feeling that encompasses grandparents who are privileged to spend such time with their grandchildren. What an opportunity this presents to share a trip to the library, the park, a movie, or to church, or just to talk around the dinner table. This is your moment to use your experiences and knowledge to the fullest. Cherish your grandchildren—who knows how and when your words will impact a decision they make in the future?

Your reward for playing all these roles may come early as a grandchild hugs you and says, "I love you," or it may come later in life when a grandchild expresses thanks for all you have done.

Grandparents' Rights and Responsibilities

1. Your home is your castle—you decide when to put the drawbridge down.

2. In your home your rules apply, not those of others.

3. You have the right and responsibility to pass on the family history and tradition, as well as Christian faith and values.

4. You have the responsibility to pass on the wisdom gained from living.

5. Your estate is yours—it is solely your decision whether to spend it or to leave all or part of it to your heirs.

6. You have the right not to be a cheap baby-sitter. However, helping out while enjoying your grandchildren can be a blessing and an opportunity to carry out the many roles of a grandparent.

7. You have the right and responsibility to show your grandchildren how to age gracefully and to demonstrate how a Christian prepares for and ultimately returns to the home office.

Senior Living

We've spent this whole chapter talking about *how* seniors can live. But what about *where* we will live in our retirement? This is a question many seniors will face. The decision likely will be based on a series of factors, including where the children and grandchildren live, which activities interest you, climate, taxes, cost of living, health facilities, church, educational opportunities, crime rates, and access to means of travel. Here is an overview of the factors to consider and the types of housing available to seniors.

Money Magazine, Retire with Money, and other such publications rate cities and states for retirement living. Traditionally, the favorite states for retirement have been Florida and Arizona because of their mild winters. However, many seniors now prefer the Carolinas and Arkansas over the severe summer heat in Florida and Arizona. Some who are more affluent spend the winters in a mild climate and return north for the summer.

There are exciting new developments in senior housing in anticipation of the soon-to-retire Baby Boomers. One such development is retirement communities on or near college or university campuses. Indiana University and Penn State University have created such communities, and other institutions of higher education are joining the trend. These communities allow seniors to take advantage of the cultural, sports, educational, and social opportunities of the campus and give the universities a valuable human resource in the seniors. A wonderful synergy can develop as seniors teach, serve as guest lecturers, or in other ways serve the university community while benefiting from the resources a college campus provides. This can be especially rewarding if the seniors are alumni of the institution.

A number of senior communities are in development all over the country, many gated for security. They often have golf courses and other recreational facilities. Some even have shopping and health facilities on the grounds. Senior living facilities are becoming increasingly complex and the terminology may differ some from state to state. Here are some generally accepted definitions.

- **Assisted Living**—A retirement living facility where services such as assistance in bathing, taking medications, and dressing are provided. This is an intermediate level of care for a person who cannot live independently but is not in need of nursing care.

- **Continuing Care Retirement Communities (CCRC)**—Also known as Continuing/Life Care Centers. These facilities usually offer a variety of independent living options for residents coupled with full medical and nursing services. Most are self-contained communities offering educational, recreational, and dining facilities, as well as shopping, banking, grooming (beautician/barber), and transportation. CCRCs usually charge a partially refundable entrance fee, as well as a monthly fee for services.

- **Hospice Care**—Home care for those who are terminally ill. Admission to a program is normally for those with no more than six months to live. Services usually include pain management, nursing care, assisted living help, and volunteers to assist the family with transportation, sitting with the patient, etc.

- **Intermediate Care Facilities (ICF)**—A facility providing care for those who are not bed-bound and who can move about on their own, even in wheelchairs. Patients here may be incontinent and need intermittent nursing services.

- **Nursing Homes/Centers or Skilled Nursing Facilities (SNF)**—Facilities for patients requiring 24-hour nursing care. Medical treatment is offered under supervision of medical doctors and licensed nurses. These centers are state-licensed.

- **Residential Care Facilities**—Sometimes called Adult Care Residences or Domiciliary Care Facilities. These are residential-type homes licensed to care for a relatively small number of residents who are able to take care of themselves in a protected environment. They provide assisted living services, if needed, and often provide care for mentally or physically challenged seniors. These facilities are state-licensed.

- **Retirement Communities**—Communities designed for those who are totally independent (or nearly so) and want to live with other seniors. These communities offer amenities such as organized social programs, dining, transportation, recreation, and access to health and shopping facilities. Some will offer assisted living services if needed.

The variety of options and financial arrangements—some subsidized by Medicare and Medicaid, others not—presents difficult choices. Study the options carefully, read all the fine print in the proposals, and obtain legal advice before making a long-term commitment of any kind.

If you are contemplating a move from one state to another, vacation or rent a home in the new community for a while to decide whether you like it well enough to commit. Some seniors do not anticipate the trauma involved in leaving friends and relatives. Make sure you are prepared (and willing to uproot) emotionally. And remember that every move costs money, so be certain before committing to a major move.

If you are concerned about deteriorating health, consider a Continuing Care Retirement Facility. You can begin in a cottage or apartment and live independently for as long as you are able. Should you need assisted living or nursing care, it is available in the same complex—usually with predetermined financial arrangements because of your previous residency in another area of the facility. The equity from the sale of the family home often is enough to buy into such a community. The equity you put in is often at least partially refunded to your estate upon your death, and the monthly charges you pay provide some meals and other needed services.

The living arrangements available to seniors continues to grow in variety, cost, and complexity. Some facilities are in magnificent locations where anyone would find living a joy. Carefully study the options available, resist strong sales pitches, sample the living arrangements if you can, and do not sign any legal agreements without careful study and legal advice. Make sure this is what you want for the rest of your life. (For more information on the living options discussed here, please see Appendix D.)

four

FINANCES

The Principles of Handling Money in Retirement

The love of money is a root of all kinds of evil. (1 Timothy 6:10)

It's been said that you can retire successfully when your income exceeds your needs. There is truth in that, but it doesn't end there. To be successful financially in retirement, you must protect (and grow) financial resources, accommodate emergencies, and provide for an orderly transfer of assets at death. Never has there been more, and better, information to do this than today.

Retirement should be a time when finances are not a serious problem. If you plan wisely, you will have enough income from social security, pensions, and investments to live comfortably. If not, there are many ways to supplement your retirement income. First, let's look at some principles for handling money in retirement.

Principles for Handling Money in Retirement

- **It all belongs to God.** The Christian's attitude toward money and worldly possessions is that we simply hold these things in trust for God. This attitude shouldn't change in retirement. We are charged to use what God has entrusted to us for His work.

- **Don't worry about money.** "God will provide." That's a promise Christians have come to rely on. It's no different in retirement. This doesn't mean we should not budget, plan, and be frugal. It means we shouldn't worry about it because our heavenly Father will take care of our needs.

- **Plan and budget wisely.** It is simply good stewardship to plan ahead and to budget wisely, even if you are wealthy. God did not give us financial resources to waste or engage in "conspicuous consumption." Christians are known for modesty, humility, and generosity.

- **Save all you can, and give all you can.** While we can't take it with us, we *can* give to others and work to spread the Gospel here on earth.

Give all you can. No one ever saw a
hearse pulling a U-Haul.

- **Get out of debt and use credit cautiously.** Retirement should be debt-free. Credit should be used carefully and be saved for emergencies. Credit cards should be paid off monthly and any debt carried into retirement paid off as soon as possible.

- **Set goals.** Set annual financial goals and track your net worth on a regular basis so you can better manage your fiscal health and Christian stewardship.

- **Seek good advice.** Finances can be complicated, even in retirement. How you dispose of your estate at death is complex, even with relatively small estates. Estate tax issues can be confusing. It is, therefore, necessary to get solid, objective advice from a Christian financial advisor or attorney who specializes in wills and estates. Beginning on page 115 are some Christian resources and ideas for finding a financial planner, should you need one.

- **Provide for the orderly distribution of your estate.** A will is a must for any retiree so his or her estate will be distributed as desired. If you don't have a will, the state in which you lived will distribute your estate according to law. If you have a large estate (worth more than $700,000), you'll need to do some tax planning and possibly set up a trust to avoid unnecessary taxes.

If You Need More Money

If you enter retirement with less money than you need, you may wish to supplement your income. There are many ways to do this. Here are some options.

1. **Continue working.** Many employers would be glad to keep good workers beyond the normal retirement age on a full- or part-time basis. Businesses get experienced, dependable workers and often, if you are on Medicare, do not have to pay full benefits. Job sharing—where two people share one job, each working part-time—is also growing in popularity. Part-time jobs are widely available for seniors who need or want to work. Jobs in retailing are plentiful and allow you to meet new people, though these jobs do not pay well. If you know how to use a computer and the Internet, there are many jobs that allow you to work from home.

2. **Start a business.** Many seniors start their own businesses. Some convert former avocations into vocations. A hobby such as woodworking, painting, photography, or catering might be

converted into a money-making business with a little effort. Many senior professionals start part-time consulting careers. Remember, Colonel Sanders started Kentucky Fried Chicken after he retired because he liked chicken and had a great recipe.

Note: If you begin taking social security before you are 65 years old, you are limited in the amount of wages you can receive without giving some of your social security earnings back to the government. Here are the limits.

Age	Amount You May Earn without Penalty	Amount of Social Security You Must Return
62–65	$10,080	$1.00 for every $2.00 over limit
65+	Unlimited	$0.00

At age 65, you can earn an unlimited income. Congress changed these regulations in 2000 and reduced the age of unlimited earnings from 70 to 65. If you want to check this or other social security information or current laws, you can reach the administration at 1-800-772-1213 or **www.ssa.gov**.

3. **Do a reverse mortgage.** Many mortgage lenders now offer "reverse mortgages," allowing seniors to take monthly payments of the equity they have built up in their homes. The lender, in effect, buys the home back from the owner and agrees to make monthly payments to the owner as long as he or she lives. This alternative should be exercised with caution if

you are not a financial expert. In effect, you have sold your home to the bank and they are paying you in installments. When you die, the home becomes the sole property of the mortgage lender. Any contractual agreement for a reverse mortgage should be reviewed carefully. The National Center for Home Equity Conversion (NCHEC) is a nonprofit association that provides help in this area. Visit its website at **www.reverse.org**.

4. **Use your home equity for income.** Another possibility is to take out your home equity and use it to supplement your income. For example, if your house is paid for and worth $150,000, consider selling it and moving into a less expensive home. A condominium, mobile or manufactured home, or a townhouse costing $50,000 to $75,000 would allow you to take the surplus equity, invest it, and increase your monthly income for life by $465 to $625 a month. (This is a rough estimate based on the ability to reinvest the equity safely at 7.5 percent interest.) If you are over 55, the federal government allows you to take out up to $125,000 of home equity without paying taxes on it. This can be done only once in a lifetime by an individual or married couple. If you do it a second time, you will have to pay tax on the full amount. But taking advantage of this "one-time offer" from the government and adding the monthly income might be just the thing to allow you to live debt-free with more financial flexibility.

5. **Cash in life insurance**. Many life insurance policies have cash values—you can receive cash payments for turning in the policy. Since life insurance for seniors is less important than for younger workers who are insuring their earnings, cashing in a policy might make sense. Check with a trusted financial planner or your insurance agent to make sure this is a viable option for you. Generally, seniors don't need to carry large life insurance policies unless the policies are used in estate planning or are necessary to provide funds for a surviving spouse.

Prudent Planned Living

In our senior years, we can live prudently and give to help others. So we can't travel or enjoy ourselves? Yes, we can, but consider carefully the witness conspicuous consumption gives to others. As good stewards of the financial gifts God gives us, we will enjoy adequate housing and transportation, even in our senior years. The material status symbols aren't important because we have the only status that truly matters—membership in God's family through faith in Jesus Christ.

He who dies with the most toys is still dead.

The Christian senior can budget, live well within his or her means, save, and give to help others. Developing a simple annual budget to plan your expenditures and plotting your annual net worth are two of the most important financial planning tools. One plans your living expenses and the other tracks your net worth so you can spot problems and do estate planning wisely.

Following are some simple forms you can photocopy and use in your financial planning. Form A is a simple budget tool you can use to plan your annual expenditures. The last line in Form A should show a surplus. If it shows a deficit, you either will have to adjust your spending or dip into financial reserves to cover it.

"To get what you want, first create a list of compelling and meaningful goals. Next, draft a dynamic plan of action, then follow through with consistent maximum effort. If that doesn't work, just cry."

Looking at your annual spending is important, but even more critical is keeping your eye on the bigger picture—your net worth. Net worth measures your overall financial situation by calculating your total assets and liabilities. Review this calculation at least once a year (on January 1, for example), and plot the data over the years so you can get a good handle on your overall financial health.

Net worth is the best overall picture of how you are doing financially. From year to year, this figure should grow at least at the annual rate of inflation. If not, your net assets are decreasing relative to their purchasing power. It is important in retirement not to let your assets diminish relative to inflation or you run the risk of outliving your assets. If you are wealthy or have no interest in leaving an estate to children or family, this is somewhat less important. Even if that is the case, it is a figure you should know for your financial planning. Plotting your net worth also will give you a better idea of how much you can give to God's work above your regular tithe. Use Form B to calculate your net worth.

Form A

Annual Family Budget

Expenditure Items	Last Year's Actual Amounts	
Food (15.7%)*	_____	(12%)**
Housing (28.5%)	_____	(25%)
Clothing (5.4%)	_____	(4%)
Entertainment (4.6%)	_____	(4.6%)
Healthcare (11.7%)	_____	(12%)
Insurance & Pensions (4.6%)	_____	(5%)
Taxes (5%)	_____	(15%)
Transportation (17.3%)	_____	(3%)
Charity (2.9%)	_____	(10%)
Utilities (4.0%)	_____	(4%)
Other (0.3%)	_____	(5.4%)
Total (100%)	_____	**(100%)**

*Percentages in this column are amounts spent by the average retired American family.

**Percentages in this column have been adjusted to represent the average retired, *tithing* Christian family.

New Year's Projected Amounts

_____

_____

_____

_____

_____

_____

_____

_____

_____

_____

Income Source

Wages   _____

Social Security   _____

Pensions, IRAs   _____

Investments   _____

Other_____   _____

Other_____   _____

Total Income   _____

Total Expenditures   _____

Surplus (Deficit)   _____

Form B

Net Worth Calculation

Assets

CASH

Checking Account _____

Savings Acc't, CDs _____

Money Mkt. Funds _____

Total _____

SECURITIES

Stocks _____

Bonds _____

Mutual Funds _____

Total _____

REAL ESTATE

Residence _____

Vacation Home _____

Investment Property _____

Total _____

OTHER ASSETS

Business Interests _____

Debts Receivable _____

Vested Pensions _____

Collectibles _____

Life Ins. Cash Value _____

Annuities Survival Value _____

IRAs _____

Other_____ _____

Total _____

PERSONAL

Automobiles _____

Home Furn./Jewelry _____

Boat _____

Other_____ _____

Total _____

TOTAL ASSETS _____

Liabilities

MORTGAGES

Residence _____

2nd Mortgage _____

Vacation Home _____

Invest. Property _____

Total _____

OTHER DEBT

Auto/Boat Loans _____

Bank Loans _____

Broker Loans _____

Other Loans _____

Total _____

CONSUMER DEBT

Credit Cards _____

Charge Cards _____

Other _____

Total _____

TAXES

Federal _____

State/Local _____

Total _____

OTHER _____

_____ _____

_____ _____

Total _____

TOTAL LIABILITIES _____

TOTAL ASSETS _____

MINUS TOTAL LIABILITIES _____

EQUALS NET WORTH _____

Investments

If you have an estate and/or excess income, you will want to invest at least some of it. There are many ways to invest, but there are also risk factors. Generally speaking, when you invest, the higher the risk an investment presents, the greater the opportunities for a higher return. The problem for the retiree is that losses of investment capital are more serious. Losses in youth can be made up more easily than in our senior years. So it stands to reason that seniors should take fewer investment risks than middle-aged and younger investors.

But becoming too conservative in investing also can be a mistake for a senior. If you have an estate of any size and are not a well-educated investor, seek advice from someone who is. We will provide general advice here, but we recommend you get help from a registered financial planner. (*Note from the Publisher:* The following information is for illustration purposes only and should not be construed as investment advice.)

Here are some sample investments by risk categories.

Low Risk

Certificates of Deposit
Treasury Bills & Bonds
Money Market Mutual Funds (MFs)
Savings Bonds
Tax-deferred Annuities
Savings Accounts

Medium Risk

Income Stocks
Utility Stocks
Real Estate Investment Trusts (REITs)
Blue Chip Stocks
High-quality Corporate Bonds
Municipal Bonds & MFs
Real Estate

High Risk

Growth Stocks
Junk Bonds & MFs
Small Cap MFs
Oil & Gas Partnerships
Collectibles
Penny Stocks & MFs
Gold & Precious Metals

As you get older, the percentage of high-risk investments in your portfolio should diminish and the percentage of low-risk investments should increase to prevent loss of capital. Your aim should be to preserve capital and, at the same time, grow your estate by a sum greater than inflation. Each case is different; the information given here will not apply to everyone. But a good mix of investments for seniors might include

	Age 65–75	Age 75+
Low-risk investments	50%	65%
Medium-risk investments	30%	25%
High-risk investments	20%	10%

Over a 10 to 20 year period, based on past performance, you can expect various investments to grow annually at the following percentages:

Growth Stocks	12%
Commercial Real Estate	11.9%
Blue Chip Stocks	10%
Long-term Corporate	5%
Bonds	4.4%
Treasury Bills	3.5%
Average Inflation	3.1%

Personal Investing

You may wish to do your own investing or you may want to have others do it for you. A major trend is the growth of mutual funds. There are now more mutual funds than stocks listed on the New York Stock Exchange.

With mutual funds, you pay experts to manage the money you invest in the fund. There are now numerous mutual fund "families" that offer specialized mutual funds for every investment need. Vanguard, Fidelity, T. Rowe Price, Smith Barney, and Putnam are some of the mutual fund "family" names you will find listed in nearly every financial section of American newspapers. Most of the fund families also have websites where you can get information on their funds as well as financial advice. Be warned: Their advice is aimed at selling their own mutual funds. It may not apply to all situations.

Mutual fund families differ in the expenses they charge and some are more successful than others. Check them out carefully before investing. Look at the one-, five-, and 10-year record of the fund you are considering compared to similar funds. Also check their expense ratios. The Vanguard Funds have the lowest expenses of any mutual fund family, but not all their funds are top performers.

Walking with God is far better than riding in a limousine without Him.

Money Magazine is perhaps the single best magazine for someone wishing to stay on top of personal investing information. The website is **www.money.com**. *Money Magazine* also has a newsletter, *Retire with Money,* which offers information for those who are retired or near retirement. There also is a portfolio of mutual funds the magazine recommends for those on retirement income.

Financial magazines such as *Money Magazine* and *Business Week* have data on the leading funds in nearly every issue, and at least once a year they rate all the funds. If you want to manage your own investments, there is a wealth of information in books, articles, and on the Internet, as well as in workshops, seminars, and courses, some developed especially for seniors. Your local community college is a good place to start looking if you want to learn more about investing.

Investment Clubs

One fun way to do some investing during retirement is to join or start an investment club. Such clubs give seniors a great way to socialize, learn about investments, and make some money. Investment clubs meet to discuss investment opportunities and to make joint investments of members' contributions—usually $20–$50 a month, depending on the club's agreement. One such senior investment club has received national attention. The Beardstown Ladies—a group of Illinois grandmothers—has supposedly beaten the Dow Jones stock average significantly over the years. The group has written five books on how to do it.

If you want information on how to start a club, the National Association of Investors Corporation has what you need. For 47 years, this organization has provided information, software, and other help to investment clubs. Its website is **www.better-investing.org**. An investment club is a great way to spend time with other Christian seniors, and you can even target your investments to Christian enterprises.

Giving

No matter what your retirement income, returning some to the Lord is part of the Christian senior's life. God didn't say, "Tithe while you have a full-time job." We give joyfully not because we are obligated but because of thanksgiving for all God has given to us—life, health, home, and, most important, Jesus our Savior.

Jackie and I have tithed since the day we were married—when we owned nothing but a beat-up Chevy. We can tell one story after another of how God met our needs. Now, 48 years later, we have more material positions than we ever dreamed of. God's rich blessings allow us to give more than a tithe in thanksgiving to Him.

As with all decisions, giving in retirement should be done carefully. As Christians, we can choose to give to organization's that are doing God's work efficiently and effectively. Before you give, research any organization to which you want to donate financial resources or time—even those claiming to be Christian. Some organizations are legitimate; some are not.

It seems our phone rings once or twice a night with some organization seeking a donation. We have established a policy in our home of saying politely that we no longer are able to respond to phone solicitations, but if they wish to send something in the mail, we will consider it. This allows us to check out the organization before giving and cuts down on the phone interruptions. If an organization continues to bother you with phone calls, simply ask them to remove your name from the calling list. They must do so by law. If they continue to call, you can take legal action against them. (To get more information about this law and how you can stop unsolicited calls, write to your state's attorney general and ask for a consumer fraud guide.)

Be wary of any organization that uses contests to raise money. If a group asks you for money to enter a contest so you can win a prize, tell them no. Unless you know the organization well and are in harmony with its purpose, do not give in this way. It's often a scam.

For 80 years, the National Charities Information Bureau (NCIB) has been working to provide information to help those giving to charities. The organization reports that in 1997, Americans gave $143.5 billion dollars to charity—85 percent of which was given by individuals. There are bound to be some thieves trying to get their hands on some of that money, so be careful. The NCIB has a free "Wise Giving Guide" you can get at its website, **www.give.org**, or by calling them at 212-929-6300. The website has a wealth of information about organizations and giving.

The Better Business Bureau (BBB) also has information on charities. Its website at **www.bbb.org** has a helpful charities information page. If you have a local charity you want to check out, you can call your local BBB and they may be able to give you information, especially if anyone has filed complaints against the charity.

As a rule, do not give to a charity with which you are not thoroughly familiar unless you have its most recent financial report. The group's administrative expenses should not be more than 15–20 percent. See how much is actually spent on the charitable program. Run from any charity that spends less than 50–60 percent on the charitable activity. No charitable organization should spend more than 50 percent on administration and fund-raising expenses. If it does, the charity being supported may be the administrators of the fund.

Insurance

Insurance needs change somewhat in retirement. We still need auto and homeowner's insurance to protect against unexpected losses, but life insurance needs may change. In our younger years, we needed life insurance to protect the family from the loss of a wage earner, usually the husband. Once the children are grown and we are living on retirement income, it is less necessary to insure the income stream unless the death of one spouse would leave the survivor without sufficient income. If this is the case, continuing a policy or retaining a paid-up policy makes sense. Taking out a new policy is more expensive as we age, so if you need to do this, do it as soon as you can and consider term life insurance, which is the least expensive.

Health insurance becomes more important in retirement because serious long-term illnesses can cause financial difficulties. At 65, seniors qualify for Medicare, which is intended to protect them from health and financial difficulties but does so only partially. With Medicare, you have the option of joining a health maintenance organization (HMO) or other managed care organization. If you do, it will most often offer benefits beyond the minimum offered by Medicare. The managed care provider frequently will offer prescription, eye care, and dental benefits subject to some deductibles. When you join, you assign your Medicare benefits to the organization and it assumes responsibility for your care up to specified limits. If you join an HMO, you must use its physicians and related healthcare facilities. You lose choices but gain additional services. If you do not join an HMO, you may need to add a *medigap health insurance policy,* which fills in some gaps and protects you from some risks not covered by Medicare.

Do you need insurance against long-term nursing home care? The wealthy can cover the costs, typically more than $2,000 a month, and the poor will have the cost picked up by Medicaid once Medicare benefits and personal funds have been used up. It is the group of seniors between the extremes that need to do some planning. Those with a net worth between $400,000 and $1 million probably should be the most concerned, particularly if there is a family history of debilitating illness in old age.

Fewer than one in three seniors will spend more than three months in a nursing home, and that percentage is decreasing. Currently, Medicare will pick up 100 days of nursing home care once in a person's life. In other words, you have a total of 100 days to be used over your lifetime as a Medicare recipient. This should be sufficient for more than 67 percent of seniors. You also can judge your chances of needing extended nursing home care from your family history. If your family has a history of Alzheimer's disease or some other debilitating illness, you may want to buy a policy. If there are no such illnesses, you may want to run the smaller risk. Extended nursing home care policies are expensive and typically will cost the average 65-year-old more than $1,000 a year. At age 70, these policies can cost $3,000 a year. Premiums can be reduced by increasing the deductibles in the policy. For example, you might agree to pick up the first 90 days out of your own funds—rather than the common 30 days—before the insurance kicks in.

Some recent trends in health care should be noted here. One is toward home health care for seniors facing debilitating or terminal illnesses. Another is toward hospice care for those with terminal illnesses. Modern medical technology and better pain management now permit some terminally ill seniors to elect to die peacefully at home rather than in a nursing home or hospital. Carefully review your situation, check current costs, and make a studied decision on whether to invest in long-term care insurance.

New and creative uses for insurance are developing all the time. One is to use a life insurance policy to provide an inheritance to your family to replace a charitable gift trust given to a charity. It works like this. You give your estate, or a large portion of it, to a charitable organization in the form of a charitable trust. You take the tax deduction for the gift now, to offset income taxes. The charity also agrees to pay you a fixed amount from the trust until you die, at which time the trust goes to the charity. You take the tax savings and some of the income from the trust to buy a life insurance policy for an amount similar to the trust to be paid to your heirs upon your death. You have, in effect, made a charitable gift and still left an estate.

A couple other creative uses of life insurance have been developed to insure against long-term health care costs. Some life insurance companies will agree to pay out life insurance before you die so funds can be used for terminal care. This can be done in two ways. There are Accelerated Death Benefits (ADB) and Viatical Settlements. ADBs usually require a rider to a current life insurance policy and provide for a lump sum or monthly payment if you develop a chronic illness. These payments may be from 25–75 percent of the face value of the policy, depending on the severity of the illness.

Viatical Settlements have been used predominantly in AIDS cases but can be used with any terminal illness. In Viatical Settlements, a company will pay you 60–80 percent of your life insurance policy, depending on how long you have to live. The company then assumes the beneficiary's role on the policy and collects the face value of the policy upon your death. The money you receive can be used for current medical expenses.

Estate Planning

Seniors need to make sure there is an orderly transfer of their estates upon death. The complexity of the task will depend on the size and type of estate you will leave behind. Larger estates also must be careful not to pay more estate tax than necessary.

A simple will should suffice for the distribution of many estates. Failure to have a will allows the state to distribute your estate and may lead to unnecessary probate fees of 5–10 percent. A simple will can be created and registered by most attorneys for less than $100—a good investment.

> Better a little with the fear of the LORD than great wealth with turmoil. (Proverbs 15:16)

If your estate is worth more than $700,000, taxes begin to become an issue. There is no tax issue, however, where a spouse is involved. One spouse can pass on any size estate to a legal mate. The issue arises when both die together or when a surviving spouse dies. The Federal Taxpayer Relief Act of 1997 currently provides that an estate of $625,000 in 1998, graduating upward to $1 million in 2006, can be passed on without paying a federal estate tax. These are per person figures, so they can be doubled for couples ($1.5 million in 1998 and $2 million in 2006). If your estate exceeds those amounts, you may wish to consider some of the legal means available for reducing the federal estate tax, which can be as high as 55 percent. You also should check into your state's position on estate taxes. Some states do not tax estates while others do.

Both husband and wife can give gifts of $10,000 a year per person to anyone, including children, without tax. For example, each parent can give each of their children $10,000 a year (totaling $20,000 per child) without any tax consequences for either parent or child. Some seniors use this practice to keep their estates within tax boundaries.

If you have an estate worth more than a million dollars, consider one

"When I was young and foolish, I thought love made the world go around. When I got older, I thought money made the world go around. Now I think it's prunes."

of the many alternatives for avoiding estate taxes. This usually involves setting up some type of trust, viewed by the government as a separate entity for tax purposes. Setting up trusts becomes very complicated. Get special help and advice.

Trusts are used also for giving purposes. There are charitable remainder trusts, revocable charitable trusts, life insurance trusts, charitable lead trusts, charitable remainder unitrusts, and many others. Use varies with individual situations and the current tax laws. Get accurate, timely Christian financial advice if you have a large estate.

It is important for your heirs to know where to find all your financial records. We suggest the following.

1. Keep an up-to-date list of assets.

2. Keep a list of where your critical papers are located, including your will, property deeds, bank account documents, insurance policies, and trust documents.

3. Write down your wishes regarding your funeral arrangements.

4. Provide a list of key people who advised you on financial matters.

5. Leave a note giving the location of keys to deposit boxes, computer passwords, and safe combinations.

6. List anyone who owes you money and where loan documents are kept.

7. Keep your will at home for easy access, but keep it in a fireproof home safe. Your attorney also should have a copy on file in his office.

8. Spell out any other wishes you may have regarding how your assets should be treated.

Doing these simple things will make the job of your beneficiaries much easier. Your legacy will be that you helped them, even after you were gone.

Financial Advice

When looking for financial advice, you may need one or more of the following.

- **Financial Planner**—Financial planners are professionals trained to provide expertise on a variety of financial issues. Some are not what they seem to be, however, so be careful. Mutual funds and insurance companies often offer free financial planning services, but these advisors have a sales agenda. The only truly objective advice will come from a fee-for-service professional who is a trained and registered financial planner. He or she will carry a CFP or ChFC designation behind his or her name and will be registered as a financial planner by the Securities and Exchange Commission. Financial planners will charge you an hourly fee for services. Many offer the first visit for free.

  The two organizations that train and register financial planners, The Institute of Certified Financial Planners and the International Association of Financial Planners, recently united to become the Financial Planning Association (FPA). The association can be reached at **www.fpanet.org**. They will help you find a financial planner in your area.

- **Certified Public Accountant**—A CPA has passed a rigid state exam and practices accounting. You may need a CPA who specializes in tax law when you are considering the ramifications of various trust alternatives. Look for one who is a Personal Financial Specialist (PFS) with expertise in financial planning.

- **Attorney**—You may need an attorney to set up your will and trusts. Talk to satisfied customers before committing to a project with any attorney. Also ask for a fee estimate and keep track of the time you spend with the attorney so you don't get overcharged.

Someone who carries the initials CMFC behind his or her name is a mutual fund specialist. The initials CPCU mean the individual is an insurance specialist, and AEP means the person is an accredited estate planner. If you have a complex estate, start with a financial planner who can help determine whether you need a CPA or an attorney. Don't be afraid to ask if he or she is a Christian before you sign a contract. A non-Christian may not understand how a Christian looks at financial and estate issues, especially charitable giving, and may not give you the advice you need. At any rate, make sure the planner explains the various alternatives open to you. Then you can carefully select the best options based on your faith and values.

DEATH

The Return to the Home Office

For the Christian, death is merely a transfer to the home office.

For to me, to live is Christ and to die is gain. (Philippians 1:21)

Why have a chapter on death and dying in a positive book on retirement? There are two good reasons. First, to a Christian death is a positive event. And, barring Christ's return, it will happen to all of us. It should be something we look forward to. Finally, we will meet our Savior face-to-face and be reunited with loved ones who have preceded us. Second, fear of death is probably the single greatest thing that robs retirement of its joy. It is essential that we come to grips with our death so we can have a joyful and productive retirement.

Billy Graham says, "Too many Christians avoid thinking about death because they think the subject is unpleasant. Death is Satan's weapon. He uses the thought of it to bring confusion and fear into the hearts of those fearing it."[7] It also has been said that if you are afraid to die, you also are afraid to live. Fear of death can cause depression and inhibit reasonable risk taking. This can rob us of opportunities to live an active and vigorous life. In this chapter, we will address that fear. We have included this chapter to present some positive perspectives that will help the Christian deal constructively with death and dying.

The Christian View of Death

One of the greatest joys of being a Christian is our assurance that Christ has risen from the dead and has returned to heaven and that we who believe in Him will join Him there after death. The Bible has hundreds of passages referring to heaven. In fact, Jesus spoke about it often.

> "In My Father's house are many rooms; … I am going there to prepare a place for you. … I will come back and take you to be with Me that you also may be where I am." (John 14:2–3)

Heaven is our eternal home and a place we all long to be. While we may have a hesitancy to leave this life and our loved ones, and while we may have some apprehension about how we will die, we should have no concern about what heaven will be like when we get there. We are assured that Christ has won for us victory over death and the grave through His death and resurrection. He longs for us to be with Him in His Father's house.

Loss of a Spouse or Close Loved One

The first reaction to the death of someone you love is emotional as well as physical shock. You may have believed you were prepared for this death to happen. You observed the changes in your loved one's physical condition. The death might have been painful. You may feel numb, hurt, abandoned, angry, and certainly lonely. Loneliness often is the worst problem for people who have lost a spouse. You no longer are able to talk with your mate about the day's events and family matters or go places with him or her. Your period of mourning can be long and difficult. Holidays may be the most difficult time as you focus on the loss of that special someone's participation in traditions. You may even ask God why this loved one was taken from you. You may think you could have done something to delay the death. You may even feel guilty because you are still alive.

People differ widely in their responses to grief. You may have difficulty sleeping, loss of appetite, periods of crying, or loss of concentration. Just getting out of bed in the morning may be difficult. It is not unusual for you to hear familiar sounds associated with the deceased such as an unusual laugh or song. This is perfectly normal.

In some instances, death may bring a feeling of relief. You may be thankful that the person is no longer suffering. This feeling of relief should not make you feel guilty and does not in any way mean there was a lack of love for the person. When a loved one has undergone weeks or perhaps months of pain, you are relieved that her suffering is over and she is in a far better place.

It is important to recognize that people handle grief in different ways. Some, particularly men, may try to hide their grief. Others may display their grief openly. It is important not to stifle your feelings of grief nor to be judgmental of how others deal with their sadness. And it is okay to cry—even for men—because tears are a natural release of tension and even a tribute to the person who died. Grieving is a natural process, and each individual needs to work through it in his or her own way.

There are things to do, however, to mitigate the depths of grief and to begin to put your life back together. Friends can be a great help. Besides your close, personal friends, support groups are available to listen as you freely express your grief.

These groups are filled with people who are also experiencing a loss. Support groups can be found at hospitals, hospices, religious organizations, funeral homes, senior citizen centers, or community mental health centers. You also may want to consult a grief counselor. Grief or bereavement counseling is a relatively new counseling specialty in which specially trained counselors assist people facing the issues of death, loss, and grieving. Different forms of physical exercise, such as walking, running, and swimming, can aid in the release of tension during the grieving process.

Children and grandchildren should not be excluded from the grieving process. Depending on their age, they need to feel a part of the situation and actually can perform useful tasks such as answering the door, helping around the house, and starting meals. Often, children are not sure how to express their feelings after a death. They will take their cues from the adults around them. Talk to them about what is going on and listen to their questions and concerns. The death has affected them, and they need your love and attention. Don't hesitate to use the words *death, dying,* and *dead* around children. The substitution of other words may become confusing and make them think that *death* is bad. Children need assurance that death is not a result of their negative thoughts, feelings, wishes, or actions. Allow them to attend and participate in the services that commemorate the life of the deceased. This is a good opportunity to teach grandchildren about how Christians view and handle death. If you would like more information on dealing with a grieving child, we recommend *The Grieving Child: A Parents Guide* by Helen Fitzgerald.

For your own well-being, don't hold back on talking about the deceased person. Talk about your memories—maybe you traveled a lot, had the grandchildren overnight on occasion, went fishing, told jokes, went to ball games, played cards, shared favorite foods. Your pain will not disappear entirely, but over time, the anxiety should fade. You might be able to laugh more, go out in public, remember wonderful times shared with your loved one. The death of a loved one is a deeply emotional experience. But your loved one always will be a part of your life. A death experience may even open up the way to new growth in your life.

> And the peace of God, which transcends all understanding, will guard your hearts and your minds in Christ Jesus. (Philippians 4:7)

After the death of a spouse, it is important for you to become active. Life must go on. God still has things for you to do or you would be in the home office too. Review the activities in chapter 3. Take a trip, meet new people, resume hobbies, volunteer for church activities. Helping others in some way often provides the best medicine.

Pets also can play a positive role in the grief process. If you don't have a pet, consider getting one. A dog, cat, bird, or some other animal can provide companionship and affection and make life better.

Some may want to seek a new mate. There are Christian dating services on the Internet for those who wish to move in this direction. Friends and relatives also may try to introduce you to possible companions. Gently and lovingly let them know what your wishes are regarding this matter so they can act appropriately. There *is* life after death, in more ways than one, even after the death of a spouse or close friend.

Dealing with Your Own Death

There are many decisions to be made prior to death. Your relationship with God will have a great impact on your actions. There are many avenues to be pursued to make your death less stressful for you and for those who will remain behind.

If you have a physically painful illness, there are health concerns regarding the use of medication and/or life support systems. You should have clear written guidelines for your physician and family members regarding what measures you want taken to make your illness bearable. Your decision to stay in a hospital for treatment or seek the treatment of a hospice organization may be considered at this time. Hospices will consider the needs of the patient through communication with family members and the physician.

Pain

When people talk about their fear of dying, one of the greatest concerns is that there will be physical pain. New medications and pain-relief strategies are being used every day to help defeat pain. Dr. Lauren Bentt, head of the Pain Clinic at the Greater Southeast Hospital in Washington, D. C., lists numerous ways doctors have to treat severe pain, including patches, lozenges, nasal sprays, shots, pills, implantable pumps, and even magnetic pillows and mattresses. No person need suffer chronic pain or lie terminally ill in significant discomfort.

Dr. Bentt also says current research shows that 40 percent of patients in nursing homes are undermedicated for pain. Most nursing homes have their own physician or medical staff. In some cases, the administrative and nursing staff do not use the medical information provided by Hospice or cooperate in pain management as they should. Many nursing homes also have their own pharmacy and might not carry the medication you need. If you run into any of these problems, insist that they get the proper medications immediately and adhere to all pain-control protocols.

There also are alternative methods to relieve some types of pain. Therapeutic massage, relaxation techniques, acupuncture, and acupressure are just a few of the alternative methods available. Do not let unnecessary pain cause you or a loved one undue suffering. Insist that pain medication be used until the pain is relieved. Many doctors and patients have voiced concern that increasing pain medication might cause a patient to become addicted. Dr. Bentt says this happens only about 1 percent of the time and should not be a concern. Any addiction usually disappears when the source of the pain goes away. Besides, some of the 1 percent who stayed addicted often had a pattern of addiction prior to the medication. If you are terminally ill with a short time to live, comfort should be a primary concern. Addiction to pain-relieving drugs should not.

Because of the variety of pain, different methods of controlling it are now available. There are now non-inflammatory medications available to relieve suffering and pain. Hospice physicians and nurses who specialize in pain control often are more experienced in treatment options than hospital staff. In fact, a study done at the Prince George's County Hospice shows that over a four-month period, more than 67 percent of patients who entered hospice care had their pain levels reduced significantly.

Adversity can make us bitter or better.

Pain can have a positive effect on the Christian. Pain can help us identify more closely with Jesus in His suffering for us. It can help us appreciate more clearly what He did on the cross. Pain can turn us to God in prayer and in supplication. As St. Paul says,

> We … rejoice in our sufferings, because we know that suffering produces perseverance; perseverance, character; and character, hope. And hope does not disappoint us, because God has poured out His love into our hearts by the Holy Spirit, whom He has given us. (Romans 5:3–4)

Pain is no longer the grim foe it once was. We need no longer fear pain. We can respect it and pay attention to the messages it sends us. But fear pain? No!

Family Members

Family members are also an integral part of your treatment in a terminal illness. Be honest with yourself and with your doctors. It is important for you to share your feelings with loved ones about your wishes regarding medications and extraordinary methods to preserve life. It is vital to set those matters into a legal framework so your wishes will be followed, even if you are not conscious or able to make decisions. This is done through the execution of two documents: a *living will* and a *durable power of attorney*. A *living will* spells out in some detail how you want things handled should you be unable to make your own medical decisions. A *durable power of attorney* delegates decision-making authority to a specific person (usually a spouse or adult child) in case you cannot make your own decisions. You need to execute both documents with an attorney. Appendix C is a document called an *advance directive*, which contains examples of both the *living will* and the *durable power of attorney*. States have different requirements regarding these documents. Check with your attorney to obtain the proper form for your state. You also may want to consult your pastor as you prepare these forms.

> "Be faithful, even to the point of death, and I will give you the crown of life." (Revelation 2:10)

If you have a terminal illness, check if your county or local hospital has a hospice unit. Hospice care at home is becoming a popular choice because you get personal treatment and improved methods for controlling pain. Nurses, under the direction of your doctor, tend to your personal health needs, primarily through medication. Health aides are available between nurses' visits. Home care volunteers assist the caregiver, freeing him or her to run errands and relieving him or her of the tension that can accompany caring for someone with a prolonged illness. Volunteers often become another friend in a difficult time.

The LORD gives strength to His people; the LORD blesses His people with peace. *Psalm 29:11*

A terminal illness may cause you to deny your illness and approaching death. Elisabeth Kubler-Ross says, "Death is still a fearful, frightening happening and the fear of death is a universal fear."[8] She also says, however, that "we may achieve peace … by facing and accepting the reality of our own death."[9]

Kubler-Ross has studied death and dying more than most. The stages of the dying process she identified are widely known and used to help people deal with death. The stages are denial, anger, bargaining, depression, and acceptance. People do not necessarily proceed through these stages in an orderly fashion, but they usually will deal with each stage in some way. Some will move forward, then return to an earlier stage. The critical thing to know is that these stages exist and that arrival at the acceptance stage will bring peace.

The cross is the only ladder high enough to reach heaven.

There are, of course, other important matters to be attended to as we approach death, including funeral arrangements, legal documents, health insurance, power of attorney, living will, bank accounts, and credit cards. Take time to review your documents annually. If you change your mind about something in your living will or power of attorney documents, for example, make the alterations right away. If you wait, the changes might not get made and your new wishes won't be carried out. We can make things so much easier on those we leave behind, if we tend to these details.

As you approach your own death, comfort those you are leaving behind. This will bring peace to them as well as to you. As your legacy, show them how a Christian faces death—with the joy and victory won through Christ.

> "Death has been swallowed up in victory." "Where, O death, is your victory? Where, O death, is your sting?" (1 Corinthians 15:54–55)

If we approach death with the clear understanding of the promises we have in Christ Jesus, are free of most pain, have taken care of administrative matters, are surrounded by loving, supporting family and friends, what is there to fear?

six

WHAT'S IT REALLY LIKE?

Retirees on Retirement

A diamond is a piece of coal that stuck to the job.

For the LORD gives wisdom, and from His mouth come knowledge and understanding. ... He ... protects the way of His faithful ones. (Proverbs 2:6, 8)

We couldn't conclude this book without sharing with you what some of the experts have said about retirement. We're not talking about the scientists who have researched the subject; we are talking about those who have lived and are living it.

When we decided to talk to retirees about retirement, we selected five groups in Maryland, Virginia, and Pennsylvania. We asked to talk to 10–12 retirees in each group who had been in retirement for at least five years. We asked the same seven questions of each group and had wonderful discussions about retirement in each place.

We should tell you that we made no attempt to get a scientifically "correct" cross-section of all types of retirees. Members in four of the groups we interviewed were in retirement communities that require some financial resources and were, for the most part, professional people with college educations.

One group consisted of seniors living in their own homes in a middle-class area. So our sampling was basically more educated, a little wealthier, and more successful in life than the average retiree. Since all of the senior groups we visited were sponsored by Christian denominations, it can be fairly assumed that those we interviewed were also more religious than the average retiree.

The ages of our interviewees ranged from 65–97 years, with an average age of 79.37 years. They had been retired from 6–33 years, with an average of 17.5 years. We looked for "experienced" retirees who had put a lot of thought into their retirement. They shared some valuable insights.

1. What is the best thing about retirement?

- Watching my neighbors scrape the snow off their cars.

- Being able to read the newspaper thoroughly every day.

- I retired to something positive.

- You have control over what you want to do—not what others want you to do.

- I am able to choose my responsibilities.

- We are able to share time together as husband and wife.

- We have more time to travel.

- My worries about catching a plane or train were eliminated.

- I am able to pick and choose activities I want to become involved with.

- I have less stress due to a schedule of my choice.

- I can now do research without the "publish or perish" threat.

- My productivity has increased.

- I can do the things now I previously didn't have time for.

- You can gain new friends.

- You can now get involved with the community by volunteering in various activities.

- My regimented routine is eliminated. I don't even have to shave or set the alarm clock.

- There's no alarm clock to wake me up.

- I can do things at my own pace.

- I can go places when there's no traffic.

    It is clear these retirees feel one of the best things about retirement is the freedom they have to do what they want. Several happily married couples mentioned that having time to do things together was the best thing for them. As we mentioned earlier in the book, this freedom is a marvelous opportunity to develop a rich variety of activities that refresh and renew our bodies, minds, and spirits but that also serve others. The key to a fantastic retirement is found in the correct selection and balance of these activities.

2. What do you like the least about retirement?

- Loss of old friends, but new friends have replaced some of the loss.

- What's not to like?

- Nothing!

- I miss some of the intellectual interaction with students and colleagues.

- We have some restriction on money.

- My physical activity is restricted in some ways.

- I actually miss putting on a coat and tie more often.

- We miss contact with more young people.

- You miss some of the old friends. Being separated from relatives is hard too.

- Your mortality is rubbed in your face daily when you reside in a retirement community.

- The boredom.

- Too many people want your time.

    It looks like there are some "down" sides to retirement. Some miss colleagues from the workplace and some the level of activity. Some feel physical restrictions and others financial limitations. But everything mentioned above can be offset to a significant degree if proper activities are selected. Exercise can help offset physical and health problems, and volunteer activities can lead to contact with a variety of age groups. A well-planned retirement can help remove many of the "negatives" some people experience.

3. What advice would you give to someone nearing retirement?

- Stay active!

- Find a hobby.

- Go to seminars on retirement.

- Continue your education.

- Exercise regularly.

- Maintain a positive attitude.

- Volunteer to help others—get involved.

- I would advise taking a course on finances and on "how to get benefits."

- You should not wait until your health fails before deciding where you will retire.

- You should plan all aspects of your retirement a few years before you are actually going to retire.

- You should carefully investigate the advantages of all retirement communities before committing yourself to a particular one.

- I wish a book on retirement had been available to us before we had to make this choice.

- You can relax. The decision [to enter a retirement community] is really not so bad.

- I found interesting activities to do now that time was in my favor.

- We chose an auctioneer to help sell possessions we had, after the children had chosen what they desired to keep.

- Don't wait until you are in your 90s before making a decision.

- We stripped down our possessions as though we were newly-weds and just starting our home.

- You should plan your retirement during the middle of your productive years.

- You should plan ahead but be flexible if something unexpected happens.

- I think some people should not retire. A retirement community is not necessarily the plan you should pick.

- I think you should not live with your children. Values today are so different.

- We found the cost of retirement communities is great. Don't leave a decision like this to your children. You should be able to adjust to new living arrangements.

- You should not wait until your health starts failing before making the decision to enter a retirement community. Don't hesitate to make a decision. You should not be worrying about your "things" and what will happen to them.

Investments
and Financial Services

GLAS BERGEN

"Squirrels don't have to save for retirement!
Birds don't have to save for retirement!
Fish don't have to save for retirement!
IT'S NOT FAIR!!!"

© 1999 RANDY GLASBERGEN.

The advice here is simple and direct. Stay active, exercise, volunteer, plan, and keep a positive attitude. Most of the seniors we interviewed also advise starting to plan for retirement early, particularly in the financial area. Each period in life has developmental tasks we should accomplish. Our retirees said, in short, to plan as early as you can, make your decisions with careful study, and don't look back.

4. What is your greatest fear as you age?

- I have no time to think of fear. Things are good.

- I fear becoming a vegetable due to ill health.

- You fear that you will not be able to continue to have a useful life.

- We fear moving to a health facility so we can be kept alive.

- I really fear a lingering illness.

- You tend to fear that the health care will not be adequate.

- I have financial fears.

- I fear being a burden to others.

Nearly all the seniors we interviewed mentioned fears

about becoming incapacitated or being a burden to others. While statistics show few seniors actually become totally incapacitated before death, it is a concern of many. We can't stress enough that one way to avoid becoming physically dependent is to develop an exercise program and engage in a healthy lifestyle. Staying mentally and physically active is good medicine. A research study recently released by the University of Michigan shows a correlation between the number of close friends a retiree has and his or her health. Those seniors with 16 or more close friends had better health than those with 10 or fewer friends.

We're not asking you to be naive. We know that some seniors do become partially or totally incapacitated. But we maintain that even these seniors can do things to help others and to remain active. They can pray for others, write letters, send e-mail, and celebrate life. The message here is to do everything you can to maintain good health, and, even if your health fails, do all you can to reach out to others, maintain friendships, and live your faith.

5. What is your greatest hope as you age?

- I would hope to be clear-headed.

- We hope we would be free of pain.

- I hope I am able to hold up to the end and handle things.

- I hope my children will not succumb to pressures of the day.

- I hope I die before my children.

- I hope to stay mobile to the end.

  Most seniors hope they will be healthy and independent to the very end. Again, how you live your life can go a long way toward making that hope a reality.

6. Has your faith in God changed as you aged?

- I have a firm foundation in my faith. There has been no change.

- No change.

- My faith has become stronger.

- I have always been an active member of my church. I believe the church has become too involved in the social issues and has let me down.

- You can now reflect on the blessings you had but didn't enjoy at the time.

- I am not functioning as I once did. There has been a sort of drifting from worship habits. I am not as devoted as my parents were.

- As I have become older, I miss the church meetings.

- My faith is an individual matter. I feel I am growing all the time.

- There is time now to reflect, do more reading.

    We were a little surprised to find some seniors hesitant to talk about their faith while others did so freely. Faith is obviously a very personal topic. It seems to us, as some suggested, that retirement is a time when your faith can deepen and the Holy Spirit can provide a marvelous peace as you near the time you will join your Father in heaven. This is the time of life when faith provides you with the resources to handle declining physical abilities and other problems of old age. While some of the seniors we interviewed did not seem to exhibit signs of deep faith, the vast majority gave evidence of strong faith.

7. Is there anything about retirement that we haven't covered that you feel should be included in this book?

- I feel in some retirement communities there isn't adequate security. Don't bring too many valuables with you. Divest of some of them, possibly giving them to your children. Seek a lawyer's advice on these matters.

- You should not fear moving to a retirement community.

- [If you are in a retirement community,] your children are generally happy about your living arrangements and don't have to worry about your care.

- You should not become a burden to your loved ones.

- Get on the computer and discover a whole new world. You also can use a fax machine or fax software to keep in contact.

- You can make new friends in your new living facilities.

- Many facilities now have daycare associated with them, thus assisting staff and residents.

So what have we learned? Plan early, stay active, live healthy, continue to live your faith, manage your finances wisely, laugh, listen to good music, and you will have the most fantastic retirement possible. It is entirely within your capacity to do so. So thank the Lord for the opportunities He gives you, and have a wonderful *refocusment!*

The Dying Person's Bill of Rights

1. I have the right to be treated as a living human being until I die.

2. I have the right to maintain a sense of hopefulness, however changing its focus may be.

3. I have the right to be cared for by those who can maintain a sense of hopefulness, however changing this might be.

4. I have the right to express my feelings and emotions about my approaching death in my own way.

5. I have the right to participate in decisions concerning my care.

6. I have the right to expect continuing medical and nursing attention, even though "cure" goals must be changed to "comfort" goals.

7. I have the right not to die alone.

8. I have the right to be free from pain.

9. I have the right to have my questions answered honestly.

10. I have the right not to be deceived.

11. I have the right to have help from and for my family in accepting my death.

12. I have the right to die in peace and with dignity.

13. I have the right to retain my individuality and not be judged for my decisions, which may be contrary to the beliefs of others.

14. I have the right to discuss my religious and/or spiritual experiences, whatever they may mean to others.

15. I have the right to expect that the sanctity of the human body will be respected after death.

16. I have the right to be cared for by caring, sensitive, knowledgeable people who will attempt to understand my needs and will be able to gain some satisfaction in helping me face my death.

Created at a hospice workshop on the terminally ill patient held in Lansing, Michigan.

25 Practical Tips to Help Those Facing a Serious Illness

When someone we know is facing an illness, especially a serious one, we often feel helpless. We stammer weakly, "Just call if you need something." Have you gotten a call lately? Here are some practical tips to *really* help someone facing an illness … from people who have been there.

1. Don't avoid me. Be the friend or the loved one you've always been.

2. Touch me. A simple squeeze of my hand can tell me you still care.

3. Call to tell me you're bringing my favorite food and what time you are coming. Bring food in disposable containers so I won't worry about returns.

4. Take care of my children for me. I need a little time to be alone with my loved one. My children also may need a little vacation from my illness.

5. Weep with me when I weep. Laugh with me when I laugh. Don't be afraid to share this with me.

6. Take me out for a pleasure trip, but know my limitations.

7. Call for my shopping list and make a "special" delivery to my home.

8. Call before you visit, but don't be afraid to visit. I need you. I am lonely.

9. Help me celebrate holidays (and life) by decorating my room or home or by bringing me tiny gifts of flowers or other natural treasures.

10. Help my family. I am sick, but they may be suffering. Offer to come stay with me to give my loved ones a break. Invite them out. Take them places.

11. Be creative! Bring me a book of thoughts, taped music, a poster for my wall, cookies to share with my family and friends, or surprise me by bringing an old friend who hasn't come to visit me.

12. Let's talk about it. Maybe I need to talk about my illness. Find out by asking me, "Do you feel like talking about it?"

13. Don't always feel like we have to talk. We can sit silently together.

14. Can you take me or my children somewhere? I may need transportation to a treatment, to the store, or to a doctor.

15. Help me feel good about my looks. Tell me I look good, considering my illness.

16. Please include me in decision-making. I've been robbed of so many things. Please don't deny me a chance to make decisions in my family or in my life.

17. Talk to me of the future—tomorrow, next week, next year. Hope is so important to me.

18. Bring me a positive attitude. It's catching!

19. What's in the news? Magazines, photos,

newspapers, and verbal reports keep me from feeling that the world is passing me by.

20. Could you help me with some cleaning? During my illness, my family and I still face dirty clothes, dirty dishes, a dirty house.

21. Water my flowers.

22. Just send a card to say, "I care."

23. Pray for me and share your faith with me.

24. Tell me what you'd like to do for me, and, when I agree, please do it!

25. Tell me about support groups such as Make Today Count so I can share with others.

Condensed from "25 Tips to Help Those Facing Serious Illness," St. Anthony's Health Center, Alton, Illinois. Our thanks to St. Anthony's and the Make Today Count group for their permission to use this material.

APPENDIX C

Note: These documents are provided as examples only. Because states differ in their language and requirements, please consult an attorney to prepare these documents.

Advance Directive

My Durable Power of Attorney for Health Care, Living Will, and Other Wishes

I, _____ , write this document as a directive regarding my medical care. (Put your initials by the choices you want.)

Part I. My Durable Power of Attorney for Health Care

I appoint this person to make decisions about my medical care if there ever comes a time when I cannot make these decisions myself.

Name _____

Address _____

Home phone _____ Work phone _____

If the person above cannot or will not make decisions for me, I appoint this person.

Name _____

Address _____

Home phone _____ Work phone _____

_____ I have not appointed anyone to make health care decisions for me in any other document.

_____ I want the person I have appointed, my doctors, my family, and others to be guided by the decisions I have made on the following pages.

Part II. My Living Will

These are my wishes for my future medical care if there ever comes a time when I cannot make these decisions for myself.

A. These are my wishes if I have a terminal condition.

Life-Sustaining Treatments:

_____I do not want life-sustaining treatments (including CPR). If life-sustaining treatments are administered, I want them stopped.

_____I want life-sustaining treatments that my doctors think are best for me.

_____Other wishes:_____

Artificial Nutrition and Hydration:

_____I do not want artificial nutrition and hydration started if it would be the main treatment keeping me alive. If artificial nutrition and hydration are started, I want them stopped.

_____I do want artificial nutrition and hydration, even if it is the main treatment keeping me alive.

_____Other wishes:_____

Comfort Care:

_____I want to be kept as comfortable and free of pain as possible, even if such care prolongs my dying or shortens my life.

_____Other wishes:_____

B. These are my wishes if I am ever in a persistent vegetative state.

Life-Sustaining Treatments:

_____I do not want life-sustaining treatments (including CPR). If life-sustaining treatments are administered, I want them stopped.

_____I want life-sustaining treatments that my doctors think are best for me.

_____Other wishes:

Artificial Nutrition and Hydration:

_____I do not want artificial nutrition and hydration started if it would be the main treatment keeping me alive. If artificial nutrition and hydration are started, I want them stopped.

_____I do want artificial nutrition and hydration, even if it is the main treatment keeping me alive.

_____Other wishes: _____

Comfort Care:

_____I want to be kept as comfortable and free of pain as possible, even if such care prolongs my dying or shortens my life.

C. Other Directions.

(You have the right to be involved in all decisions about your medical care, even those not dealing with terminal conditions or a persistent vegetative state. If you have wishes not covered in other parts of this document, please indicate them here.)

Part III. Other Wishes

A. Organ donation:

_____I do not wish to donate any of my organs or tissues.

_____I want to donate all of my organs and tissues.

_____I want to donate only these organs and tissues:_____

_____Other wishes: _____

B. Autopsy:

_____I do not want an autopsy.

_____I agree to an autopsy if my doctors request it.

_____Other wishes: _____

(If you wish to say more about any of the above choices, or if you have any other statements to make about your medical care, you may do so on a separate sheet of paper. If you choose to add a statement, put here the number of pages you are adding._____)

Part IV. Signatures

(In most states, you and two witnesses must sign and date the advance directive for it to be legal. There will be a paragraph above your signature that attests you understand the document. There will be a paragraph stating that your witnesses attest you are signing of your own free will. You will want to choose witnesses who are not related to you by blood, adoption, or marriage. Again, consult an attorney for the requirements and language necessary in your state.)

APPENDIX D

Websites for Seniors

The following websites contain a wealth of free information. In some cases the site providers also have services for sale, but you do not have to subscribe to them to get the free information. The sites listed below are but a fraction of the millions of sites on the Internet. Most of the sites below have links to other related sites. If you want more information on a topic, go to one of the search engines listed below, type in the topic, and let the search engine scan the Internet for related sites. The search engine will display a list of websites carrying the information requested.

Remember, when typing a website address, every letter and symbol must be correct, including the case of the letters, or the website will not be reached. As of this writing, every address listed here was accurate and functioning. However, addresses change occasionally and some sites are removed from the Internet by their owners. If you can't find a particular site, go to a search engine and search for key words in the name of the group you're looking for. Have fun!

Arts and Entertainment

Art Museum and Gallery Guide
www.gallery-guide.com

Movies (Times and locations of local movies)
www.moviefone.com

Performing Arts Listing
www.culturefinder.com

Playbill On-line (Lists what's playing on Broadway and in other places)
www.playbill.com

Associations and Senior Sites

Administration on Aging (Federal agency responsible for administration of the Older Americans' Act)
www.aoa.dhhs.gov

American Association of Retired Persons (AARP)
www.aarp.org

Christian Association of PrimeTimers (The Seniors Organization for Christians)
www.christianprimetimers.org

National Council on Aging (NCOA—a nonprofit association listing information and research on aging)
www.ncoa.org

Senior Search (Senior information linking to England, Canada, and Australia)
www.seniorssearch.com

SeniorCom (A company providing information to seniors)
www.senior.com

Seniors-Site (A wealth of information and links to other sites)
www.seniors-site.com

Bed and Breakfasts

The Inn Guide (Includes all 50 states and beyond)
www.inn-guide.com

Book Buying Online Services

Amazon.com Bookstore
www.amazon.com

Barnes and Noble
www.barnesandnoble.com

Borders
www.borders.com

Christian books
www.christianbook.com
www.cph.org

Careers

Lycos Careers
www.lycos.com/careers

Cartoons

Randy Glasbergen (The cartoonist who created the cartoons in this book; he posts a new cartoon every day)
www.glasbergen.com

Charities

Better Business Bureau (Rates charities on acceptable standards)
www.bbb.org

National Charities Information Bureau (Online guide to 400 charities)
www.give.org

Christian Sites

Christianity Today (with links to numerous other sites)
www.christianity.net

Gospel Communications Network
www.gospelcom.net

Religion Today (Religious news source)
www.religiontoday.com

Dictionary

Free dictionary use online
www.onelook.com

Directories

Telephone (Listings for more than 100 million U.S. residences and businesses)
www.switchboard.com

ZIP code directory and address information
www.usps.gov/ncsc

Education

New Promise, Inc. (Take college courses online)
www.mindedge.com

SeniorNet (Relates information technology to seniors; offers cruises where you can learn to use computers)
www.seniornet.org

Elder Care

CareGuide (Search for available services by state and city)
www.careguide.net

ElderWeb (Information on elder care with links to other sites)
www.elderweb.com

Encyclopedias

Encyclopedia Britannica
www.britannica.com

The Knowledge Adventure Encyclopedia
www.letsfindout.com

Family Research (Genealogical Services)

Roots Web Genealogical Data Cooperative
www.rootsweb.com

U.S. Genealogy Web
www.usgenweb.com

Financial Planners

Christian Financial Concepts (Larry Burkett—Christian financial planner and noted author of books on money management)
www.cfcministry.org

"It's called 'reading'. It's how people install new software into their brains."

Financial Planning Association (Formerly The Institute of Certified Financial Planners and The International Association of Financial Planning)
www.fpanet.org

Flowers and Gardening

Buy flowers online
www.flowerclub.com
www.ftd.com

Gardening
www.gardenmart.com

Plant Encyclopedia (Includes how to handle pests)
www.gardening.com

Franchises

The American Franchisee Association (AFA)
www.vaxxine.com/franchise/afa/afa2.html

The Federal Trade Commission
www.ftc.gov

Government Services

Federal Consumer Information Center
www.pueblo.gsa.gov

Legislative Information (Provides information on bills; has congressional directory with e-mail addresses)
thomas.loc.gov

Social Security
www.ssa.gov

U.S. Securities and Exchange Commission (Investor information)
www.sec.gov

U.S. Treasury (Internal Revenue Service tax information and forms as well as information on other U.S. Treasury offices and bureaus)
www.ustreas.gov

"My husband passed away eight months ago, but we still keep in touch. His e-mail address is WalterZ@Heaven.com"

Greeting Cards

Blue Mountain Arts (Send free electronic greeting cards to friends)
www.bluemountain.com

Health-Related Sites

allHealth (Good information and links to other sites)
www.allhealth.com

American Heart Association
www.americanheart.org

American Medical Association
www.ama-assn.org

The American Music Therapy
Association (AMTA)
www.musictherapy.com

Associates for Research Into the
Science of Enjoyment (ARISE)
www.arise.org

Centers for Disease Control
and Prevention
www.cdc.gov

The Fellowship of Merry
Christians
www.joyfulnoiseletter.com

Health Care Financing
Administration (Information
on Medicare, Medicaid, and
other programs)
www.hcfa.gov

HealthWorld Online
(Features wellness, nutrition,
and fitness information)
www.healthy.net

HealthGate (Includes health,
wellness, and biomedical information)
www.healthgate.com

InteliHealth
www.intelihealth.com

Mayo Clinic Health Oasis
www.mayohealth.org

Medicare Information
www.medicare.gov

Medscape (Extensive links to
health information)
www.medscape.com

National Institutes of Health
www.nih.gov

Pain Information—Back
(Wellness Web)
wellweb.com

Prescriptions and Drugs
(Searchable index of drugs and
medication interactions)
www.rxlist.com

Reuters Health (Reuters News
Service health information)
www.reuters.com/news

Time Warner's Pathfinder
www.thriveonline.com/fitness

Women.com (Women's health
information)
www.women.com

Insurance Information

Insurance Quotes (From com-
peting companies)
www.quickquote.com
www.quotesmith.com

Investors' Information

Invest-O-Rama (Provides links
to investment-related websites)
www.investorama.com

Money Magazine
www.money.com

National Association of
Investors Corporation
www.better-investing.org

The National Center for Home
Equity Conversion (NCHEC—
information about reverse
mortgages)
www.reverse.org

Quicken (Good information on
stocks, bonds, and mutual
funds)
www.quicken.com

Quote.com (Stock, bond, and
mutual fund quotes)
www.quote.com

Silicon Investor (Some of best
bulletin boards on stocks)
www.siliconinvestor.com

Standard & Poor's
www.personalwealth.com

United States Securities and
Exchange Commission (Filings
on companies—10-Ks, 10-Qs,
and others)
www.sec.gov

The Universal Currency
Converter
www.xe.net/ucc/

The Wall Street Journal
www.interactive.wsj.com/home.html

Yahoo! Finance (Stock tracking
and information; lets you set
up and monitor your own
portfolio)
www.yahoo.com (*under* Business and
Economy, *click on "finance")*

Legal Assistance

National Senior Citizens Law
Center (Information on legal
issues and legal assistance for
poor seniors)
www.nsclc.org

Newspapers and Columnists

AJR News Link (Links to
online newspapers all over the
world, including major U.S.
papers, as well as state and
local papers)
www.ajr.newslink.org/news.html

Ananova (For those with eye
problems, a digital newsre-
porter reads the latest news
flashes)
www.ananova.com

Drudge Report (Latest scoops
from Washington and links to
major newspapers, magazines,
and columnists)
www.drudgereport.com

New York Times
www.nytimes.com

U.S.A. Today
www.usatoday.com

The Washington Post
www.washingtonpost.com

Real Estate

*Abele Owner's Network
(Homes for sale by owners)*
www.owners.com

*HomeHunter (Links to real
estate ads in 31 daily newspapers)*
www.homehunter.com

*Realtor (List of 1.2 million
homes for sale with mapping
capability)*
www.realtor.com

Search Engines for the Internet

www.altavista.com
www.dogpile.com
www.google.com
www.hotbot.com
www.go.com
www.webcrawler.com
www.yahoo.com

Senior Living

*American Association of
Homes and Services for the
Aging (AAHSA—has a direc-
tory of CCRCs)*
www.aahsa.com

*American Health Care
Association (AHCA—offers a
free package of information on
long-term health care options)*
www.ahca.org

*Assisted Living Federation of
America (ALFA—offers a free
"Assisted Living Guide and
Check List")*
www.alfa.org

*National Association for Home
Care (NAHC—Offers a free
copy of "How to Choose a
Home Care Provider")*
www.nahc.org

Sports

CBS SportsLine
www.sportsline.com

CNN-Sports Illustrated
www.sportsillustrated.cnn.com

ESPN Sports Center
www.espn.go.com

Sports—Masters Competition

*National Senior Sports
Association (Combines travel
and golf competitions)*
www.aoa.dhhs.gov/aoa/dir/
198.html

*Over 50 Baseball (Leagues
and national tournament in
baseball)*
www.over50baseball.com

Rowing
www.usrowing.org

Swimming
www.usms.org

Track and Field
www.usatf.org

Travel

Elderhostel (Inexpensive travel, study, and volunteer opportunities for seniors)
www.elderhostel.org

Maps (Free maps of wherever you're going)
www.mapsonus.com

Microsoft Travel Services
www.expedia.com

Priceline Airline Tickets (Bid on airline tickets and get a bargain)
www.priceline.com

State Department Travel Warnings
www.travel.state.gov/travel_warnings.html

Volunteer Opportunities

Christmas in April
www.Christmasinapril.org

Habitat for Humanity
www.habitat.org

Neighbors Who Care
www.neighborswhocare.org

Prison Fellowship Ministries
www.pfm.org

Reach Out (Retired and active physicians provide care to uninsured patients)
www.reachoutweb.org

Senior Corps (Retired and senior volunteer program opportunities)
www.seniorcorps.org

Service Corps of Retired Executives (SCORE)
www.score.org

Small Business Administration (SBA)
www.sba.gov

"My high school math teacher promised that algebra would be important to me later in life. Maybe it will be on the entrance exam for Heaven."

APPENDIX E

Humor for Seniors

A cheerful heart is good medicine. (Proverbs 17:22)

The following material is provided to expand your treasure trove of positive humor. As mentioned in the chapter on health, scientific research indicates humor raises the spirit and makes for better health. As Christians, we live out the joy we have as redeemed children of God in many ways—and one way is with a smile on our faces and in our hearts. So share the laughter with friends and relatives.

As one senior said, "I can't see the forest or the trees."

A grandfather and his grandson went for a walk. The grandfather heard a frog and said to his grandson, "Did you hear the frog croak?"

The grandson responded, "Can you croak, Grandfather?"

The grandfather didn't respond. When he heard another frog, he asked, "Did you hear the frog croak?"

Again the grandson said, "Grandfather, can you croak?"

Finally, the grandfather said, "Why do you always ask whether I can croak?"

The grandson said, "Because Daddy said that if you croaked, we would get lots of money."

John and Pat were sitting outside their apartment building when a penguin walked by. "Why don't you take the penguin to the zoo?" John asked Pat. So Pat did.

The next day, John saw Pat walk by hand in flipper with the penguin. "What are you doing?" John asked. "I thought you took the penguin to the zoo."

"I did, and we had such a good time, today I'm taking him to a hockey game," Pat replied.

As they prepared for bed, a husband saw his wife taking a pill. "Why are you taking that?" he asked.

"Because it makes me feel younger," his wife replied.

When his wife had fallen asleep, the husband got up and gulped down all the pills. The next morning, his wife found him outside, sitting on the curb at the corner. "What are you doing out here?" she asked.

"I'm waiting for the school bus," the man replied.

"You're more beautiful today than you were the day I met you. You had a really big pimple that day."

"Did you know that the second thing to go is your memory?" one old friend said to another.

"Is that right?" the second friend responded. "What's the first thing?"

The first friend replied, "I forgot."

A doctor checking on three elderly gentlemen decided to test their math skills. He asked the first man, "How much is 3 x 3?"

"It's 153," the man responded.

The doctor asked the second man, "How much is 3 x 3?"

"It's Tuesday," he responded.

Finally, the doctor asked the third man, "How much is 3 x 3?"

"It's 9," the man replied.

"That's right," said the doctor. "How did you get the answer?"

The gentleman thought for a moment and said, "I subtracted Tuesday from 153."

Red Skelton, the comedian, was asked if there was ever a time when he was at a loss for words. He said it had happened only once. He had a dream that he was being brought before God. Just as he was introduced, God sneezed. Skelton said for the first time in his life, he didn't know what to say.

Why don't some senior citizens go elephant hunting? Because they can't lift the decoys anymore.

While walking in his neighborhood, an elderly gentleman was robbed by a young tough. A few weeks later the young tough saw the same gentleman, but this time he was walking a dog that looked like a dachshund. The young tough decided to rob the man again, but to be safe he brought a ferocious dog.

As he approached the gentleman, the small dog grabbed the young tough's dog, swung it around, and devoured it in two gulps. The young tough was amazed. "I can't believe what I just saw. What kind of dog is that?" he asked the older man.

"Well," said the gentleman, "before I had his nose fixed, he was a crocodile."

A golfing minister kept getting badly beaten by an elderly parishioner. One day, the parishioner saw how sad the minister was at being beaten, so he said, "Don't feel so bad. Remember that someday you will bury me."

The minister replied sadly, "Yes, but even then it will be your hole."

An 81-year-old went to the doctor complaining of a pain in his right knee.

"Perhaps your right knee is just getting old," the doctor said.

"It's no older than my left knee," the man replied.

You know you're getting old when you don't care if your wife goes out, as long as you don't have to go too.

One golden-ager told her friend, "I finally cured my husband of biting his nails."

"How?" asked her friend.

"I hid his false teeth," she replied.

How to Know You're Getting Older

Everything hurts, and what doesn't hurt doesn't work.

Your children begin to look middle age.

You finally reach the top of the ladder and find it's leaning against the wrong wall.

Your mind makes contracts your body can't keep.

You turn out the lights for economic reasons, not romantic ones.

You sit in the rocking chair and can't get it going.

Your knees buckle; your belt won't.

You're 17 around the neck, 42 around the waist, and 96 around the golf course.

Your back goes out more than you do.

The gray-haired lady you help across the street is your wife.

You sink your teeth into a steak, and they stay there.

You have too much room in the house and not enough in the medicine cabinet.

You know all the answers, but nobody asks the questions.

(List developed by Walter Cheney, Writer's Consortium, 5443 Stag Mt. Rd., Weed, CA 96094. Used with permission.)

ENDNOTES

Note: The "Sentence Sermons" used in this book are taken from *701 Sentence Sermons*, by L. James Harvey, published by Kregel Publications, Grand Rapids, Michigan, 2000.

1. Ben Carson. *Think Big.* (New York, New York: Harper-Collins Publishers, Inc., 1993), 193–194.

2. John W. Rowe and Robert L. Kahn. *Successful Aging.* (New York, New York: Pantheon Books, 1998). Used with permission.

3. Billy Graham. *Just as I Am: The Autobiography of Billy Graham.* (San Francisco, California: Harper, 1997), 720.

4. If you are unfamiliar with websites, see the section on computers in chapter 3.

5. "Forever Young?" Health Section, *Washington Post*, April 14, 1998.

6. Arthur Kornhaber. *Grandparent Power.* (New York, New York: Crown Publishers, Inc., 1994).

7. Billy Graham. *Hope for the Troubled Soul.* (Dallas, Texas: Word Publishing Company, 1991), 198.

8. Elisabeth Kubler-Ross. *On Death and Dying.* (New York, New York: MacMillan Publishing, 1969), 5.

9. Kubler-Ross, 18.